T0365520

# Drugs, Politics, and Innovation

# Drugs, Politics, and Innovation

An Emerging Markets Cocktail

AJAY GAUTAM

PARTRIDGE

**To order additional copies of this book, contact**
Toll Free 800 101 2657 (Singapore)
Toll Free 1 800 81 7340 (Malaysia)
orders.singapore@partridgepublishing.com

www.partridgepublishing.com/singapore

# Contents

*For Saloni*

# Preface

People love to travel. Ask anyone what's on their wish list and at the top would be a desire to see the world, travel to new places, learn about different cultures and languages, experiment with exotic cuisine, and dance to local music. I am fortunate to have lived and worked in almost a dozen countries across four continents, and travelled to several dozens more before I turned thirty-eight. And what I enjoy immensely is not just the differences between people and cultures, but also the similarities, the peculiarities that connect us as humans, and the desires and ambitions that transcend all boundaries.

I cannot but think how true this is in our modern-day world, as when the same sentiment was expressed by the Buddha an age ago – "In the sky, there is no distinction of east and west; people create distinctions out of their own minds, and then believe them to be true." I see this all the time around me, in places where I have lived and worked, connecting with people across ethnicities and walks of life.

It is fascinating how St. Petersburg looks and feels such a blend of Berlin and Venice; how one of the most watched TV shows ever in Brazil happens to be a soap opera based on life in India; how a bazaar in Cairo could easily be mistaken as the streets of Karol Bagh or Chandni Chowk in Delhi, and how parts of Beijing look like replicas of sections of Moscow; how the Indian movie star Amitabh Bachchan is as well known in Cairo as in Mumbai, and the *Awaara* movie songs of the late Raj Kapoor are hummed by folks in China and Russia; how all Indians know and fervently love Brazilian football players even though the country has hardly much of a tradition of playing football; how while visiting a Buddha temple in Wuxi, China, you are enchanted by the rhymes of music composed in India; and how family plays such an integral role in the lives of several cultures across the globe.

My experiences, anecdotes, and stories are mostly from the emerging countries, which is where I have spent a majority of my life. This book is an amalgamation of a series of lectures, blogs, articles, presentations, and discussions I have participated in at various forums in these markets. It is an attempt to make sense how such diverse places as India, Brazil, Mexico, Dubai, Egypt, Russia, Israel, and China – countries where I have lived, worked, or spent a significant amount of time – have some unique underlying similarities. It is also an expression of my gratitude to my wonderful friends and all the entrepreneurs from these countries that have enriched my life over the past years and decades. This is equally an effort to connect the economies between these geographies within the backdrop and insights from the healthcare industry where I have spent my entire professional career. Finally, this is a philosophical musing to unravel some of the underlying political, social, and economic paradoxes in these markets. So in equal parts it is a travelogue, a treatise on the emerging markets healthcare sector, a dialogue on the entrepreneurial spirit of these geographies, and a philosophical journey of a nomadic heart.

I often joke with friends that wherever I go some sort of economic or political event follow me. When I moved to the US from India in the late 1990s, the Internet bubble burst a few months later. When I left New York to go establish a company in Brazil in early 2007, the worst economic crisis since the Great Depression followed later that year. Soon after moving to Dubai in late 2009, the Arab Spring blossomed within a few months. I moved to Shanghai in early 2012, the same year that the once-in-a-decade political transition happened in China along with one of the most prominent political scandals in the Chinese communist party history, which was followed by a period of major turmoil in the local pharmaceutical industry in 2013. Just as I finalized one of my transactions in Russia in early 2013, a freak meteor hit a remote section of the country a couple of days after I had left St Petersburg. I hasten to emphasize that these events are a pure co-incidence rather than a sinister design on my part, and is often a source of amusement for folks I meet across the globe during my various trips.

During the boom years of the mid-2000s, there was a standing joke within the bankers globally: "If it's not Dubai, Mumbai, or Shanghai, it's Bye-Bye". Not sure how true it holds today, but I still very much love the energy and vibrancy, and the chaos, of the emerging markets and see myself actively engaged in one of these geographies for the foreseeable future. Maybe another significant event awaits me. A good one this time.

Most of this book was written during my travels around the globe, during long flights, at airport lounges, and on train rides. When I first watched the movie *Up In The Air*, it reminded me much of my life being almost constantly on the road. If my journey as chronicled here inspires even a handful of people to broaden their horizons and to go after their dreams, if it piques their interest to travel to some of these countries and triggers ideas to improve healthcare covering the gamut of emerging economies, I will consider myself accomplished.

It also behoves me to say that the companies covered in this book may have their own views on the incidents and anecdotes, and I do not wish to suggest that my representations entirely mirror actual situations. These are chronicled as my observations, and mine alone, based on having lived and worked in these countries, having either been part of or worked closely with these companies, or having interacted with people who worked for or were associated with these organizations. The cultural views are also a reflection of my time spent in these countries and are not in any way intended to offend anyone.

*Ajay Gautam*
*From an airport lounge*

# Innovation Cocktail – Emerging Markets Style

During a Q&A session, after one of my talks to an audience of students, young scientists, entrepreneurs, and venture capitalists in St Petersburg, an enthusiastic journalist asked me what Russia lacked to build a truly innovative pharmaceutical sector. In another keynote panel in Mexico City, similar questions arose from the audience on what Mexico can do to replicate a Singaporean ecosystem, if not biotech successes closer to their borders in San Diego. India, Turkey, Brazil, South Korea, and a host of other countries where I have worked, travelled, or held discussions, have similar desires. It is only in China where the discussion often veers towards *when* it will achieve innovation levels of the West rather than if, how, or the what.

Many of these countries have made concerted efforts to achieve innovation in life sciences; however, there are still no established bioclusters such as San Francisco, Boston, Cambridge (UK), or San Diego in these emerging markets. Countries like Singapore and Israel have made strong strides in that respect, with China and South Korea catching up fast, but they still lag behind the US or Western Europe in life sciences innovation metrics. A key question that comes up often in my discussions is how to build these life science ecosystems in the emerging markets. What can these countries do to bring their innovation policies to bear fruit? Why is there yet no world-class innovation hub in these geographies in spite of tremendous overall economic growth in recent decades? Are there certain key elements that are critical? How is it that some places in the world are able to foster innovation, while others fail in spite of strong efforts? This book is in part an attempt to answer these questions, evaluate and contrast the approaches key countries are taking, and what the future may hold for such efforts with respect to the life sciences industry.

*What's VITAL for Innovation?*

A framework – what I will call the "**VITAL**" model – helps understand what is needed for building successful innovation ecosystems, and I will keep visiting these elements as we move through the various geographies in the different chapters of this book. There are five key ingredients necessary for any innovation ecosystem to establish and foster:

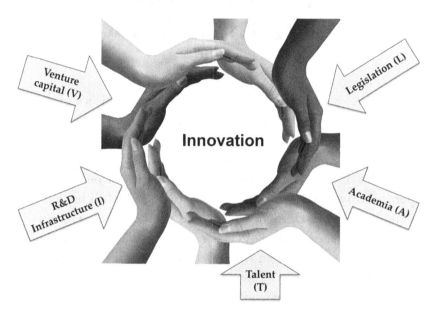

- Venture capital and funding (**V**). This refers to the levels of risk financing that flows into start-up companies, the lifeline of biotech innovation. Any start-up needs capital to grow from an idea to a sustainable and successful business, and venture funding plays a pivotal role in the early stages of these companies. In certain emerging markets, such as Russia, Brazil, and the Middle Eastern countries, the government funding bodies often play this role versus the classical venture financing in the US and Europe.
- R&D infrastructure (**I**), which refers to the quality of the clinical and medical centres, diagnostics labs, and logistical support for research activities. Countries such as Singapore, South Korea, Israel, and, to a large extent, China have built robust infrastructure to support R&D, whereas India, Turkey, Russia, Brazil, and Mexico are lagging behind in this key aspect.

- Talent pool (**T**), which is the overall quality and availability of entrepreneurs, scientists, engineers, doctors, lawyers, accountants, among others, that are available within a country to drive and support innovation. Countries such as India and China score high on this front, not just by virtue of the sheer size of the population and consequently a large talent pool, but also because of the quality and skills of the workforce, oriented as they are, towards science and technology. However, even smaller countries such as Israel, South Korea, and Singapore have been able to foster a strong scientific talent pool, despite the obvious size disadvantage, in comparison to China and India, which brings us to the next point – the quality of higher education and academia in these countries.

- Leading universities and academia (**A**). This refers to the quality of universities and research centres that are critical for producing breakthrough science. These academic centres are the engines of fundamental research and novel ideas that can then be taken through the development cycle by start-up companies or in partnership with established industry players. Most of the high-ranking universities globally are still located in the US and Europe, but several universities from China, Israel, South Korea, and Singapore are moving up the rankings globally and producing high-quality research that is often published in leading scientific journals.

- Government policies, incentives and legislation (**L**). This refers to the government initiatives, such as a progressive regulatory framework for clinical studies or reimbursement for innovative products or tax breaks for R&D, which encourages companies and entrepreneurs to develop new technologies and products. Countries such as Israel and South Korea have instituted policies that support innovation, with China catching up fast; however, countries such as Mexico and India still lag behind their emerging markets peers in this key parameter.

It is the seamless integration of these components, their inter-connectedness, that helps build a productive ecosystem, and if any ingredient is missing, the ecosystem may not provide the most optimal environment to create a sustainable innovation output. Several emerging markets are starting to incorporate various VITAL elements in their innovation policies with varying levels of success, and I will discuss how some countries have successfully implemented this, while others are struggling in their efforts to concoct this innovation cocktail.

## Political Will Drives Innovation in Emerging Markets

In an article I co-authored in *Nature* journal in September 2014,[1] I proposed a framework for classifying various emerging markets into life science innovation clusters, depending on the levels of government biomedical R&D funding and an innovation score for each country. Eleven different countries, many of which are discussed in detail in this book, were analysed and classified into the following four clusters:

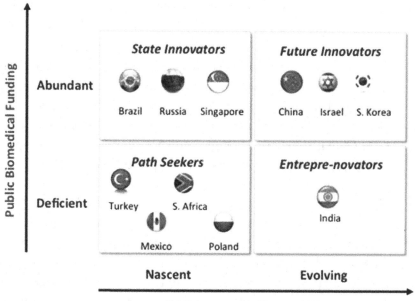

Adapted from Gautam & Yang.
*Nature Reviews Drug Discovery.* 13; 646-647; 2014.

---

[1] A framework for biomedical innovation in emerging markets. *Nature Reviews Drug Discovery.* Volume 13, 646-647, September 2014. Ajay Gautam and Steve Yang. The paper analyses 11 emerging markets – China, South Korea, Israel, India, Brazil, Russia, Singapore, Poland, South Africa, Mexico, and Turkey – and proposes a framework for biomedical innovation across these markets using funding levels and R&D ecosystems as key parameters.

- *Future Innovators* such as China, Israel, and South Korea are countries where the different elements of VITAL – funding, infrastructure, talent pool, academia, and government policy – are aligning to produce early signs of life science innovation;
- *State Innovators* such as Brazil and Russia which are relying primarily on state funding and initiatives – primarily the V (Funding) and L (Legislation) of VITAL – to build up high-tech capabilities and talent as they transition from natural-resources-driven economies towards innovation-driven ones;
- *Entrepre-novators* such as India have strong academic base, entrepreneurial drive, and talent pool – the T (Talent) and A (Academia) of VITAL – to pursue innovation that helps overcome the lack of robust government policies and initiatives (L) and financing (V) aspects; and finally
- *Path Seekers* such as Turkey, Mexico, South Africa, and Poland, which are very early in the innovation curve, as they strive to implement various VITAL elements for life sciences development.

The purpose of this book is also to offer an in-depth analysis and discussion on these different life science innovation clusters against the backdrop of my travels and work in these geographies, to delineate key success factors for *Future Innovators* and also to elucidate why certain countries have failed in their pursuit of life science innovation. It is also an attempt to connect people's aspirations and politics, and its impact on innovation, in emerging markets, using healthcare industry as a backdrop.

There are two key industry sectors of political focus and reforms across the emerging geographies – education and healthcare. And the emerging markets governments are heavily involved in both of these sectors which is a direct result of a people's desires to lead healthy lives and give their children the best foundation for a productive future. The approach various countries are taking depends on their political climate. If China is using a centralized, top-down system to create healthcare reforms and position the country as a *Future Innovator*, India is struggling on policy issues but the strong *Entre-prenovation* culture is filling the gap. Brazil and Russia are responding by using their vast capital resources from oil and natural gas as *State Innovators* to put in place policies that match people aspirations. Israel is building on its strengths in strong academic institutions, entrepreneurship, and robust government policies to continue on the innovation curve as a *Future Innovator*. The Middle East, especially the Gulf countries, is in the midst of using education – strengthening their academic centres and universities – as one of the pillars to step up healthcare innovation. And countries like Mexico are still seeking an innovation path where it can emulate the more successful emerging markets such as China, South Korea, or India. Both Mexico and the Middle East, countries such as UAE, Saudi Arabia, and Egypt, still remain very much the innovation *Path Seekers*.

The poster child of successfully implementing the VITAL framework in the emerging markets remains Singapore. This is a country that has built a truly innovative and entrepreneurial environment in the last 30-odd years. It was primarily driven by government focus on innovation and incentives (L of VITAL) – tax breaks and other incentives for R&D and the world-class infrastructure (I of VITAL) that has helped Singapore become the leading centre for biologics manufacturing, stem cell and tissue regeneration research, for example. Another aspect has been the strong academic centres (A of VITAL) such as National University of Singapore (NUS) and the collaborations NUS and other centres in Singapore have built with global universities and scientific leaders in the US and Europe. These academic centres in Singapore enjoy ample funding and grants from the government to pursue leading areas of science. This has then led to the industry participating through establishing R&D and high-tech centres in Singapore as well as regional headquarters for their Asia-Pacific businesses. And finally, the government support for entrepreneurs through start-up capital and funding plus a vibrant venture capital community (V of VITAL) has helped create a strong innovation mindset so much so that Singapore is also considered as one of the leaders in finance, banking, shipping, and other industries – not just in the emerging markets, but globally.

## Macro-factors Impacting Innovation

McKinsey, the global management consulting firm, published a study in 2012[2] showing how over the past couple of decades the economic centre of

---

[2]    Urban world: Cities and rise of the consuming class. McKinsey Report. June 2012. The report analyses how the economic growth has shifted from the US and Europe to the emerging markets over the past century, with key growth coming from countries such as China, India, South Korea, Mexico, Brazil, Turkey, and Russia. It further reviews the key cities in these emerging markets that are driving economic growth.

gravity has dramatically shifted south and east towards the emerging markets, primarily driven by the growth in countries such as China, India, Brazil, Russia, South Korea, Turkey, and Mexico. Economic and market dynamics in these geographies has also been extensively documented in *Breakout Nations*.[3] In parallel, the healthcare industry, specifically the pharmaceuticals sector, has also experienced exponential growth. According to IMS Health, a healthcare data consultancy firm, emerging market countries have accounted for majority of the global pharmaceuticals industry growth in the 2007-2014 period and key emerging markets such as China, Brazil, India, Russia, Mexico, South Korea, and Turkey will be amongst the largest markets by 2018.[4] Until 2010, only China was in the Top 10 pharmaceuticals markets globally; in 2015, six of the ten are emerging economies, namely China, Brazil, Russia, India, Turkey, and Mexico. But it is not just the economies and key industries of these geographies that have shown such tremendous growth over the past decades. What has also transpired in parallel is increasing innovation being pursued in these markets. The quality of research institutions, public and private funding, start-up activity, patent filings, and talent pool have all shown robust growth.

Where these countries go from here, and how they utilize their respective strengths, will again depend on the political environment. Consider India, for example. The new Modi government swept the 2014 national elections on the back of a strong development agenda. The social pact finally moved to where the Indian population is demanding that the government deliver on the immense talent and potential of India, rather than just let *Entre-prenovation* be the driving force. I am hopeful of many new initiatives and policies from the Modi government that will foster biomedical innovation in the coming years. In contrast, China is squarely focused on biomedical innovation as a key pillar for the future, and is in parallel implementing a huge healthcare reform across the country to distribute medical benefits to the population.[5] Having

---

[3] Breakout Nations: In Pursuit of the next Economic Miracles (2012). Ruchir Sharma. The book reviews almost two dozen emerging markets and proposes key countries that will have strong economic growth in the coming years.

[4] 'Pharmerging' markets to drive global pharmaceutical growth. (2010). IMS Health Report.

[5] Le Deu F, et al. Healthcare in china: entering uncharted waters. McKinsey & Company. November 2012. The study reviews China's healthcare reforms as a key driver of the industry growth, predicting the total healthcare spend to grow from $350 Billion in 2011 to over $1 Trillion by 2020.

achieved tremendous wealth creation and a large economic base over the past few decades, the Chinese government is focused on distributing this wealth to the broader sections of society as well as positioning the country as a *Future Innovator*. Countries such as Russia, Indonesia, and Mexico are also trying to deepen and broaden the healthcare access through national health programs and insurance coverage.

However, in spite of this tremendous progress, there remain significant hurdles and challenges. This book is thus my earnest attempt to discuss such obstacles for each of the emerging markets. The primary challenge, for me, remains the innovation culture. Several of these countries now have a strong and thriving generics industry, like in India, Egypt, Turkey, and Mexico, and to shift this philosophy from generics towards innovation will take time. This also needs an ideological and fundamental shift in our perception of science; to take risks and to allow time for progress of novel ideas. The business models and the risk funding machinery need to evolve as well. Most venture funds, private equity firms, and capital markets in these economies still look for quick returns versus the investment models of the US and Europe where capital is more patient and willing to take risks to invest in long-term R&D. An additional factor that is lacking are innovation clusters like Silicon Valley, Cambridge (UK), San Diego, and Boston where a convergence of various entities – academia, industry, investors, talent, entrepreneurial culture – come together to foster and drive new ideas. And finally, there is continued need to build talent – be it scientists, managers, lawyers, or accountants – in these geographies and to help them gain more depth in their expertise and more breadth across functions to drive, indeed nurture, the next wave of innovation.

In spite of daunting challenges, there are countries that have built on the progress over the years and have found ways to overcome various hurdles and now have evolving ecosystems capable of making the transition to sustainable innovation for the long term. China, South Korea, Israel, and to some extent, India are good examples. The way successful countries have been able to overcome challenges and build on their strengths is by nurturing and fostering a culture of innovation and entrepreneurship with a long-term view – like caring for a plant that grows into a tree and provides fruits for everyone to enjoy. And using the VITAL framework that encompasses the critical enablers to fostering new ideas, we can attempt to understand how these countries were able to build vibrant ecosystems and the lessons learned that could be used by the countries struggling to foster innovation.

## *Micro-factors Impacting Entrepreneurship*

Any innovative ecosystem is incomplete without robust entrepreneurial activity. In fact, in a *Nature*[6] paper I demonstrated – using China innovation clusters as an example – how the confluence of high academic and entrepreneurial activity fosters innovation leaders. This is very much the case with innovation hotspots such as San Francisco, Boston, San Diego, and Cambridge (UK), with a strong academic and entrepreneurial culture. This book will also discuss case studies of start-up companies from various emerging markets bioclusters, both from my own experiences where I was part of the founding team as well as from some successful and failed companies in these countries, which will help delineate the micro-environment of these ecosystems.

There are innumerable theories and guides on how to start and build a successful company. Along with the VITAL framework, I would like to share what I call the **PIPET** principles for a start-up, observed over the years from both successes and failures, and I will revisit these as I share various case studies. I have named this start-up framework after the most basic but absolutely necessary lab equipment – the *pipette* – that many of us who have worked in scientific labs have used extensively. It seems a fitting analogy since these principles are the most basic and critical ones, similar to the pipette being a basic but essential part of scientific research.

I hasten to add that these are not the only principles that are required for success – there are several other ingredients – but I have tried here to simplify the complex aspects of a start-up, more so in the rapidly evolving emerging markets. The **PIPET** framework is about the right:

---

[6]   Evolution of Chinese bioclusters as a framework for investment policies in the emerging markets. Ajay Gautam. *Nature Reviews Drug Discovery.* Volume 14, 8, January 2015. The paper analyses 8 bioclusters in China using academic and entrepreneurial intensity, and proposes investment policies for other emerging markets bioclusters such as Tel Aviv, Seoul, Bangalore, and Singapore among others.

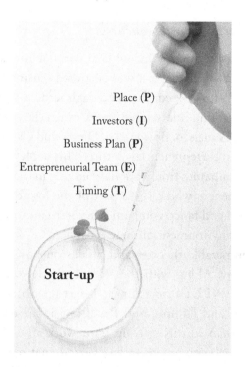

Place (**P**)

Investors (**I**)

Business Plan (**P**)

Entrepreneurial Team (**E**)

Timing (**T**)

**Start-up**

- Place (**P**), which refers to the location of the start-up. As the adage for real estate, location-location-location; so goes for biotech start-ups. There are ecosystems that are more conducive than others for nurturing companies and experimenting new business models, both across geographies and also within a specific country. The US, Israel, and UK are lot more fertile grounds for biotech start-ups as compared to, for example, Indonesia or Mexico. A Shanghai, Bangalore, and St Petersburg are again better ecosystems than a Wuhan, Nagpur, or Tomsk. This is not to say that a life science start-up can't be successful being located in non-traditional clusters, but it will have longer odds if not located in a key ecosystem.
- Investors (**I**), which refers to the angel and early stage investors who bring the financing for the start-up. An ideal investor group brings more than just capital – it provides the business networks, strategic guidance, and long term support to overcome the inevitable challenges that the venture will face, as well as the oversight and rigor for implementing the business plan. The entrepreneurial team should perform as much diligence on the investors as the financiers do on them.

- Business Plan (**P**), or the roadmap of how the start-up will achieve its vision. This is often the trickiest of the PIPET elements. In most cases, what a certain start-up eventually evolves into as a successful company will not mirror the initial business plan. There is a school of thought that argues that a business plan is not even necessary, and there's an element of truth to this. However, any start-up should think of a business plan not as a document set-in-stone, but as a compass for the end goal of the enterprise, something everyone at the firm can use to channel their energies and invest in the most impactful projects. A business plan should also build in enough flexibility to anticipate and react to external events. Which brings us to the team that is critical in this respect.

- Entrepreneurial team (**E**), which I believe is the most critical piece of the start-up puzzle. The individuals involved in starting the company, as well as the early employees, should share the same passion and vision for the entrepreneurial venture to be successful. Any start-up company will invariably face challenges, will be tested to the extreme on business competition, financing, and politico-economic volatility, more so in emerging economies. The only thing that tides the start-up through such turmoil is a cohesive team working towards a common dream, a goal to change the world in a meaningful way. The mutual trust that each team member is committed to the overall vision is critical for success.

- Timing (**T**), which is the hardest element to define and capture aptly while planning a start-up. An enterprise trying to grow during the Great Recession of 2008 or the Arab Spring of 2011, for example, would have stronger financing and political head-winds, something faced by the two start-ups I was part of in Brazil and Dubai. An e-commerce business started right after the dot-com bubble burst was probably bad timing, versus starting such business during the recent wave of e-commerce successes. Innovative, disruptive companies can often be ahead of their times, with the market and consumers not ready for their products as was the case with Sony which was the first company to launch an MP3 player or a tablet computer but did not achieve the same success Apple did many years later when the marketplace was ripe for embracing such innovation.

It is often the alignment of these key PIPET elements that helps ensure that businesses are successful, more so in the emerging markets where fierce competition, fast-changing market dynamics, and an inherent socio-politico-economic volatility require special skills to implement business strategies. And I have had more than my share of volatile situations having been part of two start-ups during times of turmoil in Brazil and Dubai.

Happy villager girl using laptop with her mother.

# It's In The Genes

India is everything it is made out to be – and then some. Often misunderstood on the outside, mostly enigmatic, unequivocally chaotic, and without doubt, the first place that comes to mind when you think of the word "Yoga". In other words, a spiritual destination for the uninitiated and a challenging place to travel and do business for ambitious entrepreneurs looking to push the boundaries. This is where the Buddha attained enlightenment under a tree in Bodh Gaya and where Steve Jobs reenergized in the Himalayas to create a dent in the world; where tradition and technology are intermeshed, mesmerizing everyone with both its sheer complexity on the one hand, and down to earth simplicity on the other.

My appreciation of India as a country, with all its nuances, the diversity of languages, customs, cultures, religions, and cuisines, came early in life as I mingled with boys and girls from across India initially during my boarding school days as a teenager in New Delhi and subsequently during my undergraduate days in Kharagpur, a small town south of Kolkata. The sheer diversity of my peers was fascinating; I was always curious about the cities and towns they grew up in, their languages, dialects and manner of speaking, so much so that I would often imitate them. I suspect this is how and why I am a polyglot; hence my comfort with, and joy for, both speaking and understanding a few Indian languages. I would enquire about the festivals they celebrate, their favourite foods, marriage customs, and the social and political landscape of the different parts of India. This curiosity in a microcosm of India during my teenage years probably fuelled my desire to learn about the global socio-politico-economic aspects in my adult life.

My passion growing up was sports, and getting into engineering, science, and business was purely accidental (or destiny, as my grandma would say). I played most sports growing up and excelled in a few such as cricket, football

15

(the one that the world plays, not the American one!), and table tennis, which I played at the school or district level. Badminton was where I excelled the most and led my district at the state championships level. But my parents pretty much put those aspirations to rest, and in hindsight, I have to say, rightfully so. India in those days was not a nation where you could make a good living playing sports, except cricket. In many ways, this holds true even today though the opportunities are vastly better now. So being the son of a scientist father and a mother who taught science in high school, the options were even clearer to me than for most Indians – to become either an engineer or a doctor, which were also pretty much the only options most Indian kids had in those days.

I did know early on in life what I might want to do and maybe that desire was instrumental in shaping my future experiences. When a teacher once asked what I envisioned myself to be as a young professional, I didn't offer the usual responses of most kids – doctor, army officer, astronaut, engineer, or an actor – no, such careers are for the ambitious ones. I proudly proclaimed I wanted to be a railway engine driver! Yes, my ambition as a kid was to drive people around in a train. Now, this is back in the 1980s when trains were still pretty much the best means of long distance travel in India and airplanes were hardly accessible to a majority of the population. In any case, while it may have appeared to most people, especially to my teachers, as a lack of ambition, deep down my reasoning wasn't all that nonchalant. What could be a better profession than to take people around all of India's fascinating cities on a train ride and get to see the country while getting paid for it? For, even as a kid, I was enchanted with the world beyond the small town I grew up in. What I perceived as a potential and promising career path died an untimely death, however, as it met with a stern and firm rejection by my parents!

My choice of an interesting career did not end there, though, much to the consternation of my parents. When I was in middle school, I tried one other profession that was cause for similar grief to my parents. I decided to launch a newspaper focused on local city news, with a sprinkling of newsworthy items from all over the nation. During those days, there were primarily two national newspapers that were available in Karnal, my hometown about two hours' drive from Delhi – *The Times of India* and *The Hindustan Times*. My parents used to get *The Hindustan Times* at home. Both were reputable and insightful newspapers, but they hardly carried the news from my small town, less so from the small neighbourhood where I resided. So I saw an opportunity and jumped right in with my plan – a few simple pages of newsworthy reportage to apprise the community of what was going on in their city, a smattering of funny jokes and anecdotes, a simple quiz section, and a sprinkling of Bollywood splash (I was, and remain, an avid Bollywood fan). Thus I launched the first handwritten edition for a very princely sum of 25-paisa, which back in the 1980s was roughly $0.06. I got lots of orders, mostly from my parents' friends, encouraging uncles and aunts that they were. Soon enough I got more orders than I could handwrite on my own, so I cajoled a couple more kids to join in this adventure and gave them a cut of the profits. Of course, I use the word 'profits' a bit liberally – what it really translated to was a few more chocolates for each of us.

Needless to say, the proverbial hell broke loose at my home! And the response here will be fascinating depending on geographies, given the cultural differences. The readers from the West would generally be encouraging of such an endeavour, and the ones from the East might frown upon it. And that's exactly how my family viewed this venture. I don't think I have seen my mom more furious in her life than on the day she found out what I was doing. For her, this was a shameful act – the fact that her son had to sell newspapers for money meant people in our community would think my parents, both well-educated and working, could not afford to give their kids pocket change. She looked at it not from the perspective of what I might want to do in life or if this little venture gave me happiness, but from the perspective of a societal ignominy. To top it off, for her I was shirking away from my main responsibility as a kid – to devote myself to my education – instead of wasting time on such a ridiculous exercise. Now, education is a key mantra for most Indian parents, if not all, and the Asian tiger moms as chronicled in the book by Amy Chua, *Battle Hymn of the Tiger Mom*[7], are a good example of what education means for Asian parents. As I reflect back now, I have to agree with my mom. The India of 1980s, and potentially parts of India even now, would have viewed my fledgling venture exactly as she did, even the uncles and aunts that I thought were encouraging might have been sniggering behind our backs. Needless to say, it was time to Stop Press (quite literally, in this case!) Otherwise, who knows if today I might have given the two national newspapers a run for their money; they might just owe my mom a lot of gratitude.

---

7    Battle Hymn of the Tiger Mom (2011). Amy Chua. The book compares the strict, disciplinarian "demanding eastern" parenting model to the laid-back "permissive western" model.

So, in many ways, this book is as much about my journey from that small town in India, from that aspiration to be a train driver to see the world beyond my city, to where I am today as an adult blessed to live that desire of experiencing all that the world has to offer; as much as it is a tribute to all the entrepreneurs who I have met in my life, who went after their dreams even though I gave up on a few of mine early on in life (thankfully, for the better!) My career preferences as a kid – linked to travel and entrepreneurship – probably also influenced my adult professional life, for I ended up being part of four start-ups across four different continents.

Once my aspirations to be a sportsman or a train driver or a media entrepreneur were squashed, I earnestly went about studying science and math to try and get admission into one of the best undergraduate academic institutions in India. In many ways, I was focused on acing the joint entrance exams for the prestigious Indian Institute of Technology (IIT). The IITs are the premier engineering institutes in India and the entrance exam for the IITs, widely regarded as one of the toughest globally, is pretty much the gold standard for academic excellence in India. Mr. Jawaharlal Nehru, the then Prime Minister of India, established the first IIT in Kharagpur in 1951 with the goal of creating an academic environment matching global standards. The IITs have lived up to the dreams of Nehru, having produced some illustrious alumni over the years – Sundar Pichai at Google; Narayana Murthy, founder of Infosys; Raghuram Rajan, governor of Reserve Bank of India and ex-Chief Economist of the International Monetary Fund; Rajat Gupta, ex-Managing Director of McKinsey; Vinod Khosla, co-founder of Sun Microsystems; Victor Menezes, Senior Vice Chairman of Citigroup; Padamsree Warrior, ex-Chief Technology Officer of Cisco – among many others. CNBC ran a high profile series in early 2000 highlighting the IITs, and even the creators of Dilbert came up with a character – Asok – for their cartoon series that was inspired by a typical IIT graduate!

The high point for me was getting into IIT; what was to come next, frankly, was more an after-thought. For me, it was mostly a sense of achievement, and also to make my parents proud after having made them go through some harrowing experiences, rather than ponder on what to become once I graduated (a theme so aptly captured in the movie *3 Idiots* which is based on the life of students at IIT).[8] But it was this initial success of getting admission to an IIT,

---

[8]    3 Idiots (2012). A Bollywood movie on the life of three college friends loosely adapted from the novel *Five Points Someone* which was based on the student life at the IITs.

something only less than 1% students get to experience, which inculcated in me a fierce desire to achieve what I wanted. The success rate for entrance into Harvard, Stanford, or Princeton in comparison is over 5%. For a small town boy, to be able to compete successfully amongst the elite of India's best and brightest provides a realization that anything is possible with a strong will, fierce ambition and yes, an ability to see beyond the windows of a railway engine.

There are several stories from the infamous IITs that have been made legendary in the movie *3 Idiots*. Here's one of my own that is as legendary, at least in my alma mater IIT Kharagpur, but hitherto unknown outside. Back in those days, we used bicycles to travel within the university campus and around the city. One evening a group of us went to watch a movie at a theatre that was about 5 kilometres away from the university. The five of us took three bicycles and on our way back from the movies stopped over at a *dhaba* (roadside restaurant) to have a late dinner. It was just past mid-night. Along with food we ordered some whiskey, rum, and cigarettes. All of us were quite drunk by the time the bill came. It was about 200 rupees more than what we all had with us combined (this is back in 1997, so 200 rupees was still a significant amount of money). Now the *dhaba* owner knew us well and agreed to let us pay the difference the next day. But we were all a bit tipsy and wanted to pay him right then. And, of course, this intoxicated desire to settle the amount right there resulted in a brainwave on our part – we decided to sell one of the bicycles to pay for the extra bill. Hell, we even got a bottle of McDowells (an Indian whiskey) in exchange for the bike after paying off the bill. We brought the whiskey bottle back to the dorm and woke up the guy whose bicycle we had just sold. He drank most of the whiskey (after all, it was his money even though he didn't know that), and we had a great time chatting until the wee hours of the morning when we finally revealed to him what had happened. Being a good sport he played along with us at that time though I am sure he was seething inside. But he did eventually take his revenge by selling my bicycle a few months later. We still remain good friends, and Sachin, if you are reading this, God bless you for being such a good sport.

Now this story is quite a shocker to many of my friends in the West and often seen as unethical, if not outright criminal. But as the saying goes in Mexico, "Mi casa, es su casa", is very much the motto in most emerging markets. As friends and family, we do take our belongings and each other for granted. In contrast to the eye rolls in San Diego or Brussels, this story is met with high fives and is cause for a toast in Sao Paulo or Moscow. No wonder the unofficial motto of my alma mater IIT Kharagpur (IIT-G) was *It's In The Genes*!

## Genes Are Ok, What About Meds!

Growing up in India also influenced my professional perspective, and I realized early in life the urgent need for better healthcare access and affordable medicines. It was probably also what drove me to major in Biotechnology and Biochemical Engineering for my undergraduate studies. The pharmaceutical and healthcare industry in India is highly fragmented, leading to fierce competition. There are hundreds of generics companies operating in India; the country has the largest number of US FDA-approved manufacturing plants in the world; hundreds of thousands of retail pharmacies across the nation; a large number of private hospital chains; and a large, though overburdened, public healthcare system with clinics and dispensaries spread across hundreds of cities and villages. However, access still remains a big hurdle. Despite a large and thriving generics business, it is estimated that as much as 50-80% of India's population is unable to access affordable medicines. Many of the villages and even Tier 3 or 4 cities lack proper infrastructure leading to supply bottlenecks for medicines, diagnostics, and vaccines.

Although a large portion of the government employees are covered through the public system, there is only a minimal private insurance system for the rest of the population making affordable healthcare a key concern for patients. This market dynamic results in a highly fragmented clinical practice where almost 50% of the physicians run a private practice or operate home clinics rather than as part of a formal healthcare system. Patients prefer and trust their neighbourhood clinics and doctors, and often self-medicate for common ailments sharing prescriptions with family or friends. The number of pharmacies in India is estimated to be in the range of 600,000-800,000, many of which are mom and pop multi-retail shops. This is probably the highest globally and, unlike for example Brazil, Mexico, or Russia, there are hardly any large pharmacy chains in India. In fact, by some estimates almost two-thirds of drugs in India are sold by the recommending pharmacists at one of these retail shops or bought by self-medicating patients with little or no input from physicians. This is a key reason often cited for the high antibiotic resistance in India.

Companies are forced to innovate on pricing and process, given the fierce competition and market dynamics in India's pharmaceutical industry, dominated as it is by a large number of high-quality generics companies. Of all the major emerging geographies, the Indian pharmaceutical market remains one of the smallest in value while ranking as one of the highest in volume due to availability of multiple generics. To place this in the right context, as per the consulting firm IMS Health,[9] the value of Indian pharmaceutical market in 2013 was roughly $15 Billion, as compared to over $30 Billion in Brazil, just under $20 Billion for Russia, and ~$15 Billion each for Mexico and Turkey. All of these countries have populations significantly smaller than India. The pharmaceutical market in China, with a comparable population to India, was valued at over $75 Billion, almost 5 times that of India.

One intriguing aspect is that the Indian generics companies have never really been successful in emerging markets like Brazil and Mexico where market dynamics are conducive. China, the Middle East, and North Africa are tough markets to enter due to local regulations, but Latin American countries should have been rich expansion geographies for Indian generic companies. One reason often cited is distance, and Indian companies have largely focused on South East Asian markets or Russia where they have had better success. Other reasons include local competition in Latin America and entrenched government relations of local companies. Allow me to present a different hypothesis, tested once with a leading Indian company senior executive. When I discussed with the executive how they chose their local country managers across the globe, the striking feature was the last name of all such general managers. Not only were they all Indian, they all had the same last name! Now, I am the biggest fan of the Indian education system, entrepreneurism, and leadership skills (more on this in the last chapter), but even I find it hard to justify that only Indians should handle a leadership role for a firm's subsidiary across different markets. Part of the reason is also that most Indian companies are family-run businesses, and this desire for control and trust perhaps makes it easier to have known managers operate the subsidiaries outside India (although, this practice is starting to shift now towards hiring of local talent). Surely there are strong Indian leaders who

---

[9]     Pharmaceutical market outlook. (2015). IMS Health Report.

may be a good fit in some countries, but to say that there are no Brazilian, Mexican, Russian, or Indonesian nationals qualified to run the respective subsidiaries is taking the nationalistic fervour a bit far.

Maybe it's *not* all in the genes!

## *Entrepre-novation*

While a fragmented market place with a predominance of generics manufacturers has made available affordable drugs to a wider cross-section of the population, the flip side is that innovation has suffered. The drive to compete on generics drug prices has resulted in companies shying away from investing in research and development for innovative drugs. Many VITAL factors are missing in India's life sciences landscape. Although Indian companies in other sectors – IT (such as Infosys, Wipro, TCS); energy (Reliance, Suzlon); automobiles (Tata, Mahindra); steel (Tata, Jindal) among others – have competed on a global scale making large acquisitions abroad and launching innovation from home, the life science industry has lacked a truly innovative global player. The number of novel molecules launched in India is also comparatively lower than many other emerging markets, as is the number of life sciences patents and comparative global rankings of research-based universities. Add to that government ineffectiveness in establishing robust policies and incentives, all of which have negatively impacted the levels of innovation, thereby failing to provide an environment conducive to the huge talent pool and entrepreneurial capabilities that the nation has to offer.

So India very much falls into the *Entrepre-novator* cluster, where innovation happens *despite of* government barriers rather than *because of* helpful state policies which is often the case for the *Future Innovators* like China, Israel, and South Korea or the *State Innovators* like Brazil and Russia. The hurdles to innovation in India due to lagging infrastructure, incoherent government policies, strong generics industry, and lack of funding are overcome by a vast talent pool and strong entrepreneurial drive. And, in spite of various challenges, there are good examples such as Glenmark Pharma or Biocon that have taken a strikingly different route from that of the majority of the Indian pharmaceutical players; these companies invested very early and significantly in the discovery of novel molecules. Now, drug discovery is a highly risky and expensive proposition, with a typical drug launch costing several billion dollars[10] and over a decade to launch with only a mere 5 out of 100 candidates ever reaching market; the rest 95 fail during the stringent preclinical and clinical phases of testing.[11] So it is even more impressive for any Indian pharmaceutical company to take such risks.

Glenmark had a humble beginning and over time evolved into one of the leading generics players in India. But for its young CEO, Dr. Glen Saldahna, who took over the company from his father, the desire was not just to launch copycats of large multinationals' drugs but also to compete and partner with them on innovative drugs. Saldahna strategically focused his company on disease areas with high unmet needs (such as pain and diabetes), invested resources towards discovering innovative molecules, and judiciously partnered out the drugs to multinational pharmaceutical companies before the most expensive clinical trials stage. In the process, he created one of the rare, successful hybrid pharmaceutical business models in India, continuing a focus on the generics business while also investing in innovative drug research. Saldahna further double downed on innovation by acquiring a Switzerland based biologics R&D unit in early 2000, which was rare for an Indian company at that time.

In a country where the stock markets tend to take a very myopic view of any cash expenditure relative to immediate revenue growth, it was admirable for Glenmark to have spent significant capital towards in-house R&D. The company's stock price initially took a hit soon after the new strategy was revealed, with the markets discounting the long-term value of innovation, focusing instead on short-term returns from expanding the generics business. But the R&D model worked out reasonably well eventually. Over the 2000-2010 period, Glenmark was able to turn R&D into a cash generator from being the erstwhile expense centre. The company spent roughly $100 Million on research of novel molecules and received $120 Million in upfront and milestones payments during that decade. This partnering model allowed Glenmark to bring in cash that could fund the R&D investments, as well as allowed the company to retain downstream value in the form of milestones

---

10   Tufts Centre for the Study of Drug Development (2014). The research calculates the costs of launching a drug at ~$2.6 Billion. http://csdd.tufts.edu/news/complete_story/pr_tufts_csdd_2014_cost_study

11   How to improve R&D productivity: the pharmaceutical industry's grand challenge. *Nature Reviews Drug Discovery*. Steven Paul, et al. Volume 9, 203-214, March 2010. The paper analyses the historical success rates of pharmaceutical R&D and strategies to improve the ~5% chances of launching a drug.

and royalties from MNC partners if the products were found to be successful in subsequent clinical trials and market launch. Multinationals such as Sanofi Group, Eli Lilly, Merck, and Forest Labs partnered with Glenmark, further validating its research expertise and business model. However, Glenmark did fail the ultimate test, one of launching novel drugs since all the partnered molecules failed in the clinical trials phase of development.

There is also significant innovation in the broader healthcare sector in India. The 'frugal or reverse innovation' is another area where India has excelled, driven largely by the dynamics of the local markets. Consider the story of General Electric. When GE engineers were evaluating an electrocardiogram (ECG) device for the Indian market, their biggest challenge was to design a portable device at an economical price point that would be attractive to both the urban and rural markets of India. The device would also need to overcome the challenges of intermittent power supply in most Indian cities and villages. The specifications and material used by an ECG device in the US made it completely unattractive for the Indian market. The engineers sitting in GE headquarters in the US would have never fully appreciated the drivers behind such needs but the local engineers at GE India were able to design the machine in a much simpler fashion. Gone were the in-house GE designed monitors, panels, printers, chips, and other high-end components that invariably increased the price and power consumption, as well as made the machines larger and heavier. GE engineers in Bangalore replaced all of this with a local solution – by using a ticket counter that is often used by bus conductors and movie theatres in India! Small, compact, and inexpensive, it provided them with a machine that could be modified to fit with the ECG specifications, run enough number of tests, *and* have a longer life for the rechargeable battery. This device not only enjoyed a runaway success in India, but was eventually launched in other markets globally.

These pricing dynamics and the inherent ability to find local solutions are what make India a fertile ground for *Entrepre-novation*. Aravind Netralaya hospital is another such example. Aravind routinely does over a 1,000 eye surgeries a day with a success rate of over 95% at a cost of a few hundred dollars. A similar surgery in the US can cost as much as $5,000 per eye and has a lower success rate. The surgeons at Aravind have perfected the science and art of performing eye surgeries, specifically for cataract, and the hospital is run almost as an assembly line with six-sigma efficiency. Another equally fascinating and similar example is that of Narayana Hrudayalaya for heart surgeries, built on the very same principles as Aravind Netralaya. Yet another pioneering and successful experiment, with a different business model in a high unmet medical need, is NephroPlus that established stand-alone dialysis clinics for kidney patients. This is very different from the traditional model of in-house dialysis wards in large hospitals. But such disruption was possible due to Vikas Vuppula and his co-founders' focus on patient care and their mission to provide a cost-effective, one-stop shop approach for kidney disease through NephroPlus.

Not just in specialty clinics, such *Entrepre-novation* is happening in the generalist hospital segment as well. Consider Vaatsalya Healthcare, another experiment in India launched by Dr. Ashwin Naik, which has built a network of cost effective primary and secondary care hospitals. These clinics, mostly in the Tier 2 and 3 cities of India, seek to provide access and affordable healthcare to the underserved populations in these towns. When I first visited the headquarters of Vaatsalya in a small nondescript building in Bangalore, I was amazed and impressed by the passion and energy of the management team. The offices were nothing of note, with piles of papers on desks, a small conference room in which we had a meeting and a simple decor, a far cry from the likes of a Fortis, Max, or Apollo hospital chains in India. The simplicity of the offices was reflected in a simple, but fascinating, experiment the team shared with us. In order to understand how salt intake impacts blood pressure and heart conditions of the Indian patients, the team planned to distribute 1 kg packets of salt per household in a Bangalore neighbourhood. Each family was asked to use salt as per their normal routine in cooking. After a month, the team would go back to each of those households and measure the amount of salt consumed by the family and take readings of their blood pressures and heart condition history. This simple experiment was designed to correlate the salt intake with blood pressure and heart condition, and provide a data set to these households to help them understand the implications of high salt intake. The same simplicity in their approach reflects in how the group built its hospitals across the country, seeking to serve the very basic healthcare access, diagnostics, and treatment needs at the bottom of the pyramid. Companies always chase the next breakthrough innovation, but often all that is needed is a little ingenuity, a little simplicity like Vaatsalya.

One interesting aspect you may have noted is that many of the stories discussed here trace their roots to Bangalore, a vibrant city in the southern part of India. As an ecosystem, Bangalore is one city in India where life sciences innovation is vibrant and thriving.[12] It is interesting to trace the roots of this, and it goes back to the early days of Astra, the Swedish pharmaceutical firm, setting up a research centre in Bangalore in the 1980s (the Astra part of AstraZeneca prior to the merger with Zeneca in 2000). Over the years Astra was the pride of the Bangalore scientific community, fostering an innovative environment and tapping into the local scientific talent pool. Many of the biotech companies that started over the years in Bangalore – Biocon, Aurigene, Jubilant, Strand Life Sciences, among many others – owe some of their success to the ecosystem that Astra helped create over the years, including the talent pool it nurtured that went on to become part of these organizations. Bangalore is also home to some of the finest research institutions, such as the Indian Institute of Science (IISc) and the National Centre for Biological Sciences (NCBS), which provide a strong talent pool. Finally, there is an angel investors and venture capital community that supports start-up activity.

Outside the healthcare industry, I always find it fascinating to study the history of the renewable energy company Suzlon and its founder Tulsi Tanti. Suzlon used to be a small textiles company. However, Tanti was not making much profit selling textiles in spite of restructuring the company to manage costs and being price competitive. Soon enough, Tanti realized that the key component of costs in his business – electricity – was highly variable and kept increasing on a regular basis. What Tanti did next transformed Suzlon into the powerhouse it is today. He closed down the textiles business and started an electric generator business to capture the market opportunity he saw – that of reliable and economic supply of electric power to businesses. Today, Suzlon is the largest wind power company in Asia and one of the largest in the world.

## What's Next for India?

There are many such entrepreneurial stories in India that started from humble beginnings. It is also this spirit of "*despite of*" rather than "*because of*" that makes India such a fascinating place. And its this *Entrepre-novation* spirit that could be the reason why India might be poised to be the innovation leader

---

[12]   Evolution of Chinese bioclusters as a framework for investment policies in the emerging markets. Ajay Gautam. *Nature Reviews Drug Discovery*. Volume 14, 8, January 2015. The paper analyses 8 bioclusters in China using academic and entrepreneurial intensity, and proposes investment policies for other emerging markets biolcusters such as Tel Aviv, Seoul, Bangalore, and Singapore among others.

in the long term, as I will further elucidate in the last chapter, comparing the socio-politico-economic aspects of the various emerging markets. A key element that is acutely missing is the active participation from the government around policies and regulations (L of VITAL) that support and reward biomedical innovation. It is this crucial VITAL aspect that I believe could be a major stumbling block that may hold India back from advancing towards being a *Future Innovator* like China, Israel, or South Korea.

# What's up Texas!

Houston is synonymous with NASA, oil and gas, and the petrochemicals industry. It was also, unfortunately, made infamous by Enron. But for me, this is the city where I had some of the most profound experiences of my early adulthood that shaped my future professional and personal life. I lived out of a car for a few months. Lost a dear friend, and saw another battle successfully with cancer. Launched a start-up that crashed even before it could take off. Tested the VITAL and PIPET frameworks in a biomedical ecosystem that interlinks them to near perfection. And the Texas Medical Centre in Houston, the largest medical centre globally, provided me with the foundations of comparing and contrasting the healthcare systems of the US and the emerging markets.

After my undergrad, I did what many of my classmates and fellow IITians did over the years – move to the US for higher education. The place I chose, though, is less popular among my college brethren. It wasn't the east or the west coast, but Texas. For a kid leaving a small town in India, going to the US came with its own perceptions – skyscrapers of New York City, beautiful beaches of California, hot bikini-clad girls of Baywatch, the glitter of Las Vegas, to name a few. And then, there's Texas!

As I walked into Houston's George Bush International airport in the summer of 1998, an elderly southern gentleman smiled and asked me "What's up"? I literally looked up at the airport ceiling first before realizing he was just saying hello. This embarrassment was rather mild as compared to the incident a friend, who for months didn't know what "paper or plastic" meant in the grocery checkout line, had to face – she always thought it was a choice to pay by cash or credit card, rather than if she wanted the groceries packed in a paper or plastic bag. Or another friend who, driving for the first time in the US, drove through the toll booth on a highway without paying since it said "EZ Pass,

No Cash". There are a whole lot more stories of us immigrants mucking it up. But there's such an innocent charm about these mistakes that you often look back and smile warmly at the early days of adapting to a culture shock. And Texas sure is a shock; it does not even seem like a part of the US. Heck, even the Texans and the rest of Americans believe as much.

Over the years, I have migrated into new countries and cities many times over but there are always the anxieties of adapting into a new culture. As much as you prepare, you are never fully ready for how the local culture, customs, environment, and people will challenge you and this is as much fun as it is demanding. These experiences have been both an inspiration and influence on my life, compelling me to share these in this book. I hope that it inspires people to move out of their comfort zone and explore all that life and world has to offer, to be entrepreneurial, to travel, to push boundaries.

## *Three Strikes and You Are Out!*

Although I trained as an engineer during my undergraduate studies, I joined Baylor College of Medicine, a leading medical school in the US, for my doctorate program. My undergraduate degree was in Biotechnology and Biochemical Engineering, a field so nascent to India that I was part of the very first graduating class with that major from IIT Kharagpur in 1998. If I wanted to gain knowledge in healthcare and medicine, I reasoned with myself, a medical school setting would be best suited to get that experience from, which could then be utilized in both basic and applied research. It also allowed me to put my engineering background to good use since my doctoral thesis was to develop aerosol-based therapies for lung cancer patients. I was able to collaborate with researchers from the MD Anderson Cancer Centre and Rice University's department of Biomedical Engineering. In hindsight, this was one of the most crucial decisions of my life that I am glad was made from a desire to follow my passion. Being in the largest medical centre in the world also allowed me to interact with students and professionals from all over the globe, further fuelling my desire to interact and learn about various cultures.

My PhD mentors – Dr. Vernon Knight, Dr. Cliff Waldrep, and Dr. Charles Densmore – were advisors and mentors in the truest sense and I am blessed to have had the privilege to train under such individuals. Their passion for science, their focus on patients was inspiring for a young student like me. They gave me the freedom and the space to pursue interesting projects, while at the same time pulling me back from pushing into too ambitious a line of research. This is more critical than a lot of people realize. A highly ambitious project is seductive for a young student, but can also be the difference between a long, drawn-out doctorate program and a realistic one. I was fortunate that my mentors helped me focus on interesting and ambitious projects, but kept me grounded enough not to go after a crazy, pipe dream. But as has been the case most of my life, I did face my fair share of glitches through graduate school.

Dr. Knight once counselled me that in baseball there are 3 strikes and you are out. I had 2 strikes and came close to a third one. My first strike was when I planned an impromptu trip to Mexico with my roommate without giving an advance notice to Doctors Knight or Waldrep. I disappeared for 5 days, literally. The school called up all my friends, and no one had a clue where I was. I didn't have a mobile phone, being a poor graduate student, so they couldn't get hold of me. Everyone in my lab was first worried, and then furious with my complete lack of professionalism and consideration. When I walked nonchalantly into my lab on Monday morning a week later, I was given a harsh dressing down and a stern warning from Dr. Knight. Strike 1! During IIT days, my attendance in class was a mere 15% – in a good year. So missing classes or not showing up was no big deal. But I had not yet grown out of my undergrad days until Dr. Knight looked me in the eye and gave me that first strike. I profusely apologized, owned up to my mistake, and was forgiven.

What I didn't mention to anyone was the reason I went to Mexico. One of my close friends, Sara Chapa, a young 32 year-old beautiful woman from Mexico, was diagnosed with breast cancer. It was thankfully diagnosed early and she was treated in Houston. This was my first run-in with a deadly disease, up close, and that too, a friend whom I cared for deeply. When Sara first told me she had cancer, I just stared blankly at her for several minutes, speechless. She was calm, composed, and was asking me how to break the news to her family. I admired her strength and was embarrassed at my own weakness, notwithstanding the fact I was a 23 year-old kid trying to come to grips with such a tragedy. I still remember the fear and anguish in the eyes of Sara's mom, a wonderful elegant lady who always treated me as her son. Sara survived the ordeal, came out stronger from the surgery and medication, and is leading a healthy life today back with her family in Mexico. But I can never forget those moments in my life when I felt I almost lost a dear friend forever.

During the weeks and months when I would join Sara for her check-ups at hospitals in Houston, I got to see the US healthcare system at work, up close.

Not ideal by any means, but the contrast between US and India were striking. The care and respect with which the patients and their families were treated, the ease of access to diagnoses and medications, and the overall interactions with the physicians and nursing staff were all enlightening. Contrasting that with India, where patients and their families were routinely given the run-around of various public or sometimes even private hospitals in those years. This was late 1990s/early 2000s, however, and the infrastructure and facilities are profoundly better now in India, but this early experience helped me realize what can be achieved by bringing in professionalism, access, and innovation to the healthcare industry in India. The fact that Sara's family members visited the US to be with her and access medical facilities in Houston, rather than have Sara go back to even the best hospitals in Mexico City, was further evidence of the huge gap between healthcare systems in the two countries. It would be almost a decade later during discussions with INMEGEN, the genomics institute in Mexico, that I realized the unique nature of breast cancer in Mexico. For genetic reasons still unclear, and something INMEGEN is working with the Broad Institute in Boston to understand, breast cancer in Mexico inflicts women much earlier in life sometimes as young as early thirties, similar to my friend. The tumour is also much more aggressive than with other populations in the world. Research from INMEGEN and Broad will hopefully soon help understand why Sara and other young women are more at risk in Mexico and how new diagnoses or treatments can help them.

My strike 1 was completely worth it; my strike 2 was an utter disaster and too embarrassing to even pen down. Thankfully, I graduated before I could give Dr. Knight a chance for a third strike. A man of admirable energy, he was in his eighties when I joined his lab to pursue my doctoral research. He graduated from Harvard Medical School and then fought during the World War II in France as a part of the US medical corps. Ever since I joined his lab, he would say that he was close to retirement and would not take on any more graduate students after me. He kept his promise to not bring in any more students, but kept working for another decade, well into his nineties, from the day I joined his group. What I didn't realize was that his definition of retirement was having fun in the research lab. After the two ignominious strikes, I can safely say I went on to make Dr. Knight proud. It was a reflection back to the days when I had embarrassed my parents with my brainwave of selling newspapers. To make them proud, I aced the IIT. To make Dr. Knight proud, I finished my PhD in probably one of the shortest possible time in the history of Baylor College of Medicine. In precisely three years as compared to an average of almost six years for the US graduate programs. And not just that, my research led to 12 peer-reviewed publications in well-respected scientific journals as compared to an average publication of 1 for PhD graduates. I received the *Sigma XI* award for meritorious research from the National Student Research Foundation as well as the American Society of Gene Therapy Award for my doctoral work.

So how did that happen? This transformation from close to three strike-outs to finishing a doctorate in three years. There was definitely a fierce desire of achievement that has always been the fire inside me, further fuelled by wanting to make a wonderful mentor proud of me. There was a huge element of luck that is so much needed in science as in life. But one other aspect that I learned from Dr. Knight, among many things, was to love your job and give it everything you have. I emulated Dr. Knight to the best of my ability. I worked hard on my thesis, often spending most of my time in the lab. I would walk in around 10am and often leave the campus after midnight. There were innumerable nights I slept in the lab and would be woken up by the cleaning staff early in the morning. But I loved every single moment of those long, often lonely periods of research because I was passionate about my work, knowing how it could impact lives of patients. I am indebted to Dr. Knight for my entire life for fuelling this passion and inculcating in me such work ethics during my student days.

After graduating from my PhD program, I was at a crossroads about what to do next. I loved science, had published extensively on my research and was passionate to pursue it further. But as is the case in life, there was a turning point in my scientific career. This came about when the aerosol therapy we were developing was partnered to SuperGen, a California-based pharmaceutical company. The company bought the commercial rights to the cancer therapy and would go on to take it through clinical trials and potential market launch. I was involved with Doctors Knight, Waldrep, and Densmore in several of the discussions and presentations to SuperGen and was intrigued by the business aspects of science. Dr. Knight, an insightful observer of people, soon encouraged me to think of the pharmaceutical industry as a career path rather than academic research. Maybe he also felt I just wasn't cut out for academia, though thankfully he never told me that. My other advisors, Doctors Waldrep and Densmore, were equally supportive. This second pivotal decision in my life, again taken more from a mix of gut feel, guidance from trusted mentors, and following my passion, further changed the course of my life. I applied for business school at Rice University and started soon after completing my PhD thesis.

## *J&B: Jim & Boxer*

Just a few months before I was to graduate from my doctoral program, I met Jim Vaughan, an elderly gentleman in his eighties, who was looking to rent a room in his house. Jim was in a wheelchair and I volunteered to help him with daily chores and care for his dog, a Dachshund I used to call Boxer. In exchange he waived my rent for the room, which was a good bargain helping me save much-needed money to pay for my business school tuition down the road. I loved having long chats with Jim over a J&B scotch, his favourite brand along with Jim Beam bourbon, in the evenings and weekends. We shared a similar rapport as the one in *Tuesdays With Morrie*,[13] just that for Jim and me it was for the whole week and not just an hour every Tuesday.

Jim worked for the US government all his life and always had interesting stories from Iran, Iraq, and the Middle East where he served during the 1960s and 70s. He provided me with rich perspective and insights into the Middle East, its culture, customs, politics, and business. This would be invaluable to me later on in life when I lived and worked in the Gulf and North Africa. I would often invite my friends over for lunch on the weekends so they could meet with Jim. It was always such a delight to see the spark in Jim's eyes chatting with my friends over scotch and beer and sharing stories from his life around the world. Maybe it was this spark that inspired me to share some of my own stories from around the world as a tribute to my dear friend.

Jim was wonderful; an inspiration the way he lived his life to the fullest until his last day, a true friend and family that I missed and needed as I started a new life challenge in the US. He was so proud that I was about to graduate, step into a professional career, and build on my life's dreams that I had often shared with him during our evening chats. He planned to be at my graduation and had even picked out a nice suit for the occasion. But a few weeks before my graduation, Jim decided to go in for knee surgery; he desperately wanted to

---

[13]    Tuesdays with Morrie (1997). Mitch Albom. A memoir by Mitch Albom recounting the time he spent with his 78-year old sociology professor Morrie Schwartz who was dying from ALS.

walk again, take Boxer for a walk in the mornings, and not be dependent on anyone. Knowing his age and condition, I advised him against it. Something in my gut didn't feel right; I was afraid to lose someone I had become so close to, more so after Sara's cancer scare. Jim never came out of the operating room. That whole night, and for the next few days, Boxer ran around the house looking for him. It's been well over a decade but I still can't forget the look in Boxer's eyes, looking for his friend and pleading with me to somehow find Jim. I realized in that moment of sadness the true meaning of a man's best friend, and I myself pretty much only had Boxer to share this hollow feeling of loss.

My experiences with Jim also brought home a harsh reality of life and ageing, and the comparison between the emerging countries and the US. One aspect is the old-age care facilities in the US. There are several centres across various cities where senior citizens can reside together and enjoy the twilight years of their life. However, given atomized families in the US, most senior citizens are left to fend for themselves. In emerging markets, be it in India, China, Philippines, or Egypt, there are hardly good facilities for old-age care, but the families often rally together to support senior citizens. Traditionally it has been more of a cultural imperative rather than an economic one. This delicate balance is unfortunately getting ruptured in many countries now, especially in the metropolitan cities like Mumbai, Shanghai, Sao Paulo, or Cairo where nuclear families are increasingly the norm given fast-paced lifestyles, limited apartment space, and social values that are becoming more westernized. Oftentimes, demanding careers of dual-income professional households and material ambitions drive the next generation out of their native cities and hometowns. This leaves the older parents to fend for themselves, even in erstwhile cohesive, extended family cultures like India and China. My dad's own battle with Alzheimer's disease, and our family's struggle to cope with this in India where the social and medical understanding of this disease is minimal, heightens this for me – bringing such conflicts to the forefront, reinforcing my passion and desire to continue working towards enhancing healthcare in the emerging markets.

Jim also happened to be the guy who helped me get through the logistics of getting to attend business school. I had the admission letter from Rice University but, before I could start attending the classes, the school needed a bank statement with sufficient funds to get through the first year of tuition and living expenses. It amounted to roughly $30,000 and my bank account was nowhere close to that; I had precisely $7,000 saved from my three years of

PhD stipend and giving tuitions to students. And so I found an enterprising solution. I requested Jim, and three of my friends from IIT days – Manda Hemanth, Vikram Kanodia, and Asheesh Chibber – to loan me money for exactly twenty-four hours. My account showed the requisite amount during the period in which I created a bank statement for the school and the money was then wired back to Jim and my friends. I was rich, for precisely a day, and then was back to a poor, struggling student. I owe tremendous gratitude to Jim, Manda, Kanodia, and Chibber for their help during that time. Much of what I am today is in many ways owed to such wonderful friends I have had in my life.

So let me spend some of this chapter discussing how I managed to go through business school without much debt in the hope that this can inspire some students to emulate my journey, hopefully much more smoothly.

## Suitcases in a Honda

The first car I bought in my life was a second hand 1988-model Honda Accord. True to the immigrant mentality of going for reliability, I settled for a safe Japanese car. The adventures of owning this 'safe' car were quite unique though. The sunroof's rubber lining leaked water during the rains (which is quite a bit in Houston) and, of course, I had completely missed this small detail when buying the car. I still remember having to ask one of my dates to open up the small umbrella I had in the back seat of the car so that she wouldn't get soaked from the leaking roof. But that was not the worst part about my reliable means of transport. The gearbox broke at one point and was broken for several weeks given my lack of finances to fix it. So there was no functioning reverse gear and I could only drive the car forward. I had to park in places where I was sure to be able to drive out front rather than by reversing. One of my dates never understood why I would not park in completely open slots but go around the parking lot for ten minutes looking for something – she jumped out and ran when I told her the car had broken gears! Needless to say I never saw her again. Fortunately I was living in Houston where you could still find such space; this would have been impossible in New York or San Francisco. Oh, and you could only use one piece of electronics in the car at any single point of time. If you used the AC, the music system wouldn't work. If the music was on, you couldn't roll down the power controlled windows.

For all my misgivings, I still miss my first car.

There are moments in life when we are greatly humbled, often in private reflection and sometimes in public. Jim's passing brought one such moment for me. Within a few days, not only did I lose a wonderful friend and the closest thing to a family in the US, but I was also without a home, literally. I didn't have much belonging; don't even now since I have always been a minimalist. My old broken Honda was my makeshift apartment for the next few weeks and I had just enough clothes, books, and a blanket to fit in the car. Oh yes, and my umbrella for when the roof of my 'apartment' would leak in the rain! I was fortunate to be living in Houston where it doesn't really get cold and my university parking area was large enough to find an inconspicuous spot. I used the gym shower facilities in the mornings, and 'ironed' my shirts and trousers by the steam of the hot showers – a handy trick that I have used when traveling and staying at hotels with no irons. I would just take my trouser and shirt to be 'ironed', keep it close to the hot running shower and let the steam take the wrinkles out. Just had to be careful to avoid the water dripping on to the clothes (it did happen occasionally, though).

Try it sometime. Worked for me!

In business schools globally, often the image is more important than substance, unlike engineering or science Masters and PhD programs. My days living in the car brought home that point quite starkly. Often I would feel helpless, embarrassed if my classmates would come to know of my misery, and a tad bit fearful as to what the next day or week held for me. Ironically, I was also carefree in some sense. This has got to be the worst, I kept telling myself. There's not really much more of a bottom left here, literally. Today, my friends often ask me about my minimalistic nature and how I am happy and content with so little even though I can very much afford many luxuries. I have hardly shared my 'living out of a broken car' experience with anyone, but those days still remind me of the beauty and satisfaction of a simplistic life. The less baggage you have in life, literally and figuratively, the easier it is for you to enjoy all that the world has to offer. My old beat-up Honda has also been a metaphor for the journey of my life – leaving one city and country for the next one every few years, ready to face ever-new challenges and opportunities with little more than two suitcases that can fit into the trunk of a Honda.

Even though Jim had always offered me the use of his brand new Cadillac to go to school – and, more importantly, to pick up dates – I had politely turned down the offer. Not that I didn't *want* to drive a nice car, but I did not want to *get used* to a nice car. I also could never afford the gas mileage of a Cadillac versus my Honda. Driving my old beat up car reminded me of my struggles and didn't let me get too ahead of myself; driving Jim's fancy Cadillac could have made me take things for granted that I could ill afford.

After a few weeks of camping in the Honda, I eventually moved to a small garage apartment next to the university since I had to sell my car to pay for tuition. Yep, that trinket still had a good engine and got me some handy cash. I managed to find a small studio on top of a garage of a house owned by the university and convinced (maybe begged, but I don't remember) the treasurer office to rent it to me for $50 a month. Not kidding, and which, by the way, I soon enough negotiated down to $25 a month! The studio had its own shortcomings, though. There was no shower or hot water, and the room would shake when a car was being parked in the garage downstairs. Oh, and you could not have more than 3-4 people in the room at the same time without being in real danger of the floor falling through. The positives were that the place was a mere five-minute walk to school and I could still use the university gym for showers. The other advantage, a big one for a cricket buff like me, was that there was a big open backyard that was promptly converted into a cricket field by my buddies and me for weekend games of competitive local cricket.

## Scrappy Dreams, Debt Free

I had jumped into business school excited, but not comprehending the full scope of the challenges. Though I had managed to save a bit of money over my three years of PhD stipend, the tuition and living expenses for the two years' business school program were still several tens of thousands of dollars. Since I was paying for tuition in business school and was always short of cash, I started working part-time teaching math and science to students in high school, community college, and university undergraduates. The most enthusiastic were always the Korean and Chinese parents, who wanted their kids to be the best and cajoled me to push their kids hard during the teaching sessions. Often I wondered how I came across to these children and was amazed to realize it was probably the same way I used to think of my mom, a strict teacher always pushing us to be at the top of the class.

Many years later, I would read the book *Battle Hymn of the Tiger Mom* and realize even more vividly how my students must have felt about me.

Normally a business school student in the US walks out on graduation day with tens of thousands, often in excess of a hundred thousand dollars, in debt. I somehow managed to keep my debt levels on day of graduation to close to zero. I am not sure how I managed to pull it off but hopefully some of my reflections here can help innumerable students in such situations. It was always my single-minded focus, resilience, and perseverance that I believed were instrumental in achieving my goals. But in this case there was one other key element that I believe played a prominent role – I had no plan B. I never considered what might happen if I couldn't pay my tuition, what if I didn't have enough money for food or rent, for books, clothes, or anything for that matter. That lack of plan B left me with no choice but to do whatever was needed to pursue my goal – to be "scrappy" – whether it was to give tuitions, use old books from the library to study, often have just one meal a day, live in a car, so as not to fail in my ambitions. I walked into business school with $7,000 in savings; over the next two years of my MBA program, I fully paid for the tuition and all other expenses through part-time work, and walked out with no debt. And this lack of debt also gave me another choice, to again go after my dreams rather than be bogged down by looking for a cushy job to pay off the debt. I could just follow my passion and take risks unlike many of my friends and peers in business school that had to contend with paying off their loans. This "economic freedom", so aptly captured in the lecture of Prof. Deepak Malhotra[14] during his Harvard Business School speech to the graduating class of 2012, is what I have striven for throughout my life.

An episode during my business school interviews for Sabre Holdings, a Fortune 500 company that owns Travelocity, reminds me of the unexpected turns of my life. I had just come out of a great interview and Sabre selected me for the final round to be held the next day. However, Ali Rizvi, a close friend who also interviewed with Sabre was not on the shortlist. Now what I did next is something only someone who grew up in India, or one of the emerging markets, may be able to comprehend. I went to the interviewers and asked if they could replace me with Ali in the final interview since he would be a better fit for the company. The interviewer was shocked and didn't know what to say. They didn't do what I had requested and asked me to come back for the final interview the next morning. My interview was spent mostly with Sabre folks trying to understand what was going through my mind to do such a thing. I

---

[14]  Speech to the 2012 graduating class of the Harvard Business School. Deepak Malhotra. In this speech, Malhotra implores graduating students to "quit early, quit often" until they find their passion.

did get the final job offer with Sabre as a financial analyst, which I declined to go work for a start-up. But Ali and I still share this warm moment until today and laugh about it. I did this in an attempt to help my friend who I genuinely felt was a better fit for the job, but what also allowed me an opportunity to do this was that my scrappy dreams had left me debt free to take more risks in life.

I still remember the times during business school when I couldn't join buddies out for drinks or a night out since finances were thin and I slept little between classes and tutoring. But those days were also some of the best of my life. Funny how life sometimes is so paradoxical, isn't it? Here's another paradox. Once you go through such hard times, a normal response would be to get more conservative. Get through school, land a cushy job, and hunker down. What did I do after all the tough times I had been through? I declined a Fortune 500 company's offer, and went for a no-name, risky start-up as my first job. Partly because I still had this desire to be in entrepreneurial settings from my childhood, and partly because there was nothing to bog me down from taking the risk.

## *Houston, We Have A Problem!*

The start-up business was fundamentally a sound one. Houston happens to have the largest medical centre in the world, is amongst the top US cities in terms of National Institute of Health (NIH) funding comparable to the San Francisco Bay Area and Boston/Cambridge. It has some of the best medical schools, clinical, and research institutions such as Baylor College of Medicine, MD Anderson Cancer Centre, University of Texas, Rice University, University of Houston, and Texas Children's Hospital, among several others. But unlike Boston or San Francisco, it has no vibrant biotech industry. Often people are hard-pressed to name even a single biotech company from Houston that made it big on a US or global scale, unlike the east or west coasts each of which boasts of many such companies. Several attempts at kick-starting a biotech industry in Houston, including setting up a biotech park in Woodlands area of north Houston, were largely unsuccessful. So our team started a company, aptly named Momentum BioVentures, on the hypothesis that there is a tremendous opportunity to tap into the innovation from the Texas Medical Centre, supported by local and state government incentives, to build a biotech sector. At a minimum, our team felt we should be able to facilitate translation of lab research into commercial biotechs within Houston. We started exceptionally strong – our Board Chairman was Steve Miller, ex-CEO of Shell Oil; board members included Frank Young, ex-FDA chief under Presidents Bush Sr. and Clinton, as well as Kirby John Caldwell, who was pastor to the Bush family. Funding was lined up, deal flow was strong, and our own networks within the scientific and academic communities in Houston were exceptional. The team had a great mix of experienced entrepreneurs such as Chris Efird, CEO, who was a serial entrepreneur; strong scientific expertise in Dr. Upendra Marathi with a deep network within the Texas Medical Centre scientific community; Susan Vick, one of the finest fund raisers in the business; Joe Rozelle, a finance whiz; and rookie out-of-school enthusiasts such as yours truly. But eighteen months into forming the company, we were about to shut it down.

My first big lesson in professional life was about failure – that of my first company, my first start-up, and my first job, all of which happened to be the same. Often in life we learn a whole lot more when we fail; when successful, we gloss over the reasons for success since we are busy enjoying the glory. When we fail, it's quite lonely and you have a lot of time at hand to ponder over what went wrong. As Dr. A. P. J. Abdul Kalam, the late President of India, aptly put it "Don't read success stories, you will only get messages. Read failure stories, you will get some ideas to get success". The lessons learned in my first start-up in Houston proved to be invaluable to me over the course of my professional career, and let me share with you my failure story to also illustrate the interplay of VITAL and PIPET frameworks in the case of Momentum BioVentures.

In the case of Houston, many of the VITAL elements were in force. The city boasts of strong universities and a sound research base (A of VITAL), robust NIH funding and local government initiatives (L of VITAL), and R&D infrastructure (I of VITAL). However, two key elements were missing. One is a vibrant venture capital investing environment in life sciences – the V of the VITAL – which lags significantly behind that of San Francisco, Boston, San Diego, or Seattle. Our team viewed this as a hurdle but also as an opportunity for our investment fund. But the lack of competition we envisioned locally was a misguided concept. In a fairly inter-connected research world, the new ideas and discoveries from Houston institutions were as accessible to the venture funds on the east and west coast as they were to Momentum negating any significant local advantage we had. We often saw these opportunities go outside of Houston to the more established bioclusters.

Another, more critical, factor was the industry base that could potentially provide a ready pool of management talent – an aspect of the T of VITAL – that can rotate around and start companies. This is an element that is present not just in San Francisco or Boston, but also around the Connecticut/New York/ New Jersey/Philadelphia region given the large presence of pharmaceutical firms along the I-95 corridor. If the east coast had Pfizer, Merck, Novartis, Johnson & Johnson, Bristol Myers Squibb, among others, to provide managers and experienced drug developers who could translate east coast universities' ideas and technologies into companies, the west coast had experience emanating from Roche/Genentech, Amgen, Lilly/Hybritech, Johnson & Johnson, and Novartis, among others. Even the hub of Research Triangle Park (RTP) in Raleigh/Durham, North Carolina, had a large presence of GlaxoSmithKline. If you remember, in our Bangalore example discussed earlier in the India chapter, there was AstraZeneca facilitating the ecosystem. Houston was the only major city with a large concentration of medical schools, hospitals, and universities that had no Big Pharma presence (Big Pharma refers to the large multinational pharmaceutical companies). As we built Momentum BioVenture's business and efforts to invest in the Houston area companies, we found out quickly how hard it was to recruit senior executives to the city. Their preferences were always towards San Francisco, Boston, New York, or San Diego where there were more opportunities to interact with peers as well as robust career prospects for their significant others. Interestingly, the Houston weather was often also cited as a key hindrance to attract managers.

Which brings me to the start-up success framework. The main aspect of what failed for Momentum was that we completely underestimated one of the P of PIPET – the *Place* of our business. It's not to say there weren't other reasons, including a less than ideal execution of our strategy and operations, but a large driving factor was likely that we were in Houston versus a San Francisco or New York for such a business idea. The large concentration of venture firms with academia, talent pool, and entrepreneurs, along with a strong industry presence, is a big factor in the vibrancy of the east and west coast innovation clusters. To replicate such an overall environment in Houston, in spite of the presence of several strong factors, will probably take a long period of time. Almost fifteen years after our failed experiment, and many more such efforts from others, Houston is unfortunately no closer to achieving that status.

## US Model for Emerging Markets

The US remains the gold standard for biomedical innovation globally, and is a model being emulated by many emerging geographies. The desire to create a San Francisco or a Boston, or even a struggling Houston-style ecosystem, is strong for countries such as China, South Korea, Egypt, Mexico, and others. The entrepreneurial spirit of the US – that indomitable culture of rewarding risk-taking – is hard to replicate easily. However, many of the VITAL elements are being put in place across emerging markets – be it strong academia, government policies, building talent pool, R&D infrastructure, or venture capital funding – to support ecosystems across Shanghai, Bangalore, Istanbul, Seoul, Tel Aviv, and St Petersburg, to name a few, that can compete in biomedical innovation with a San Francisco or Boston. The next few chapters will discuss how each of the emerging markets is attempting to put in place the various VITAL elements, how such efforts are bearing fruit, and what key aspects are still missing.

A picture of the famous sugar loaf mountain in Rio de Janeiro. It is one of the most visited tourist spots in Brazil.

# Start-up Samba

When one thinks of Brazil, 4S's come to mind – Surfing, Samba, Soccer, and Sex – not in any particular order, but your guess of the reverse order would be a good one. I traded one 'S' for another – a Start-up. I will let you speculate which of the original 4S's I traded for the start-up. Of all the countries I have worked and lived in, I have a soft spot for Brazil although the unique culture can present some business challenges. The laidback culture and business norms can be disconcerting for many, but that passion and zest for life, if skilfully channelled, can provide wonderful results as was the case with my start-up in Brazil.

Brazil is also one of the most ethnically diverse countries in the world. There are Caucasians, mostly of European descent from Portugal, Italy, and Germany; the indigenous population of Brazil; Middle Eastern, primarily from Lebanon; a significant Jewish descent; and a large Japanese population. In fact, the highest number of Japanese in any city in the world outside of Japan is in Sao Paulo. If you take a walk through the streets of Liberdade, a district in Sao Paulo city, you will be greeted with rows of Japanese shops and restaurants, street signs in Japanese characters, and people speaking Japanese, almost giving you a feeling of being in Japan (with a more chaotic environment, of course, as compared to Japan). I will actually go out on a limb here and claim, much to the consternation of my Japanese friends, that some of the best sushi restaurants in the world are actually in Sao Paulo, even better than those in Tokyo.

This fascinates me – the emigration trends not just in Brazil but also across the globe. And I have attempted to study this through my life and work travels across the world. Another interesting trend is the Indian emigration to different parts of the world. Given it is such a diverse country within itself, it's fascinating to see how different communities in India from its disparate states have emigrated across the globe. You will find a large number of immigrants from the southern state of Kerala in Middle Eastern countries such as UAE, Saudi Arabia, and Oman, to the extent that Malayalam, the language of Kerala, is now a semi-official language in Oman. Singapore has a large immigrant population from Tamil Nadu, another southern state of India, while South Africa and Kenya have a large immigrant population from the western state of Gujarat. In the UK and Canada, there is a large representation from Punjab, while Silicon Valley in the US has a substantial population from the IT hub of Andhra Pradesh in India. Such trends are also visible among other ethnicities, be it Vancouver in Canada with a large Hong Kongnese population, or Israel, where roughly 20% of the Jewish population is from Russia (both of these though for very different political reasons as compared to the Indian emigrants).

There also happen to be strong cultural links between Indians and Brazilians. I personally couldn't have chosen a better time to be in Brazil. The year 2007 marked a time for Brazilian television that was running a TV series called *Comino de India* or the "Ways of the Indians". This was a soap opera on the life of an Indian family, played by Brazilian actors and actresses. It followed the lives of these family members, their eating habits, their costumes, culture, marriages, music – basically recreating India for Brazilians through a TV series. As they say, life is all about timing. I happened to land in Brazil just when this TV series was the biggest show ever on Brazilian television. Never before was socializing so effortless for me. Locals, especially Brazilian women, would come up to me and ask about India, and whether *Comino de India* correctly depicted Indian life. But this also made me reflect on what is precisely so fascinating about Brazil. The country is so far away from anywhere in the world that for most Brazilians, even today when the world is so connected, what really brings home the world to them are such television series. Every few years, Brazil TV launches a series on different countries of the world. Before India it was Lebanon; prior to that Turkey. It just so happened that, luckily for me, it was India in 2007 that became one of the biggest hits in Brazilian TV history and I stood to bask in the glow of such a fortunate occurrence. Needless to say, I was never short of female attention or cocktail conversations during my time there just by virtue of my genetics – remember, *it's in the genes!*

## Starting a Company, in Between Soccer and Surfing

Brazil and India also share similarities with regards to strong entrepreneurial companies and home-grown conglomerates. An interesting case study is

Votorantim in Brazil, one of Latin America's largest enterprises. There are several similarities between Reliance Industries of India and Votorantim. Both companies started as family businesses, established their leadership primarily in oil and gas initially, and then expanded into consumer, telecommunications, healthcare, and even venture capital. They play prominent roles in their respective countries, and both harbour global ambitions having firmly established themselves in home territory. Coincidentally, both Reliance and Votorantim partnered with moksha8, though I would say it was the result of smart deal making on our part.

I was fortunate to be part of a team that started a company by the name of moksha8 based out of Sao Paulo, Brazil.[15] The early days were typical of any start-up. We were a team of 6-8 people with an energetic CEO, hardly any office space, and a blank sheet of paper with grand ideas of conquering the world, all backed by Texas Pacific Group (TPG), the world's marquee private equity group. The company had an amazing culture, driven in large parts by Simba Gill, the CEO – competitive, fun, dynamic, and fast-paced. And what further spiced up the start-up was the exotic Brazilian touch.

We identified a niche opportunity within the Brazil and Latin America pharmaceutical industry that our team was able to capture quickly. I go back to the key PIPET principles here. moksha8 was able to leverage each of those criteria quite efficiently, which underscored the basis of its success. The company grew from scratch to over 200 people with operations in both Brazil and Mexico over the course of the three years I was there. It was even more successful after I left; though, I hope, *in spite* of me leaving rather than *because* of. Of course, we had our fair share of hiccups. We came close to be driven out of business several times, but the team held on to its core beliefs and was able to deliver on its business goals. Watson Pharma, which later merged with Actavis, first acquired significant equity in the company in 2010. Eventually, Forest Labs followed and acquired a large equity stake in 2012. Actavis and Forest merged in 2014, and we often joke that moksha8 played matchmaker to the consummation of these two companies.

Each of the PIPET elements worked well in the case of moksha8. We were in the right *Place (P)* with the right *Timing (T)* – Brazil's pharmaceutical sector was still in its early growth phase during 2007. Multinational companies were

---

15    Quagmire to goldmine? (2008). The Economist. The article reviews the launch of moksha8 and its business model in Latin America.

primarily focused on China, and to some extent India and other parts of Asia. Latin America was pretty much off the radar, although it represented a ~$50 Billion opportunity back in 2007 and was valued at over $100 Billion in 2013. Our entrepreneurial team (E of PIPET) included seasoned and experienced pharmaceutical industry operators and local stalwarts such as Mario Grieco, who served as the General Manager of our Brazil and Latin America operations. He previously headed Bristol Myers Squibb for Latin America and had also served as healthcare advisor to President Lula of Brazil. Our board members included the likes of Mohand Sidi-Said, ex-Pfizer Head of International Markets, who had managed in excess of $10 Billion of revenues in his role; Davinder Singh Brar, ex-CEO of Ranbaxy who built the company from scratch to an $8 Billion enterprise; and William Meaney, CEO of Invida, the largest pharmaceutical distribution company in Asia. The financial investors (I of PIPET) included the ~$50 Billion, San Francisco-based private equity powerhouse TPG and the ~$10 Billion Brazilian conglomerate Votorantim, as well as venture capital group Montreaux Equity Partners from San Francisco. Further validating our strong business plan (the other P of PIPET) were partners such as Roche and Pfizer, leading global pharmaceutical companies. The team was then able to turn all these great aspects into a sustainable business.

Partly inspired, and partly serendipitous, we also found a niche business segment at the right timing (the T of PIPET). We were able to adapt our business plan to quickly capture this local opportunity. Given the robust profit margins of large pharmaceutical companies and strong growth still being experienced in the mid-2000s, several players such as Pfizer, Roche, Merck, and Novartis were not actively promoting their mature products. These mature products are characterized as those drugs that have lost patent protection. But given the high-quality brand name of these mature products among physicians and patients alike in Brazil, sales of these products were still strong with either flat to low single-digit growth or, at worst, a modest decline. A little bit of context here: in pure generics markets such as US, Germany, and India, once a product loses patent, sales go into a tailspin, often declining by as much as 90% within the first year of patent expiry. Our hypothesis was that by putting some marketing muscle behind these brands in Brazil, we could grow the sales, and the partners (multinational pharmaceutical companies and moksha8) could split the profits generated from this uptick in sales as compared to the flat or declining trend under the current 'no marketing' scenario. Given the strong brand name of moksha8, reputed financial backers, and the experienced management team, we were able to quickly establish ourselves as the partners of choice in this market segment.

However, there were several challenges the company faced over the years. I still remember the very first deal we finalized with Roche. At the time, moskha8 did not have a single person hired on the ground in Brazil. Although Mario had committed to joining the company, for confidentiality reasons we could not disclose to Roche who our general manager was to be once the deal closed. Take a moment to think about it – here we were trying to convince a leading multinational to hand over almost $50 Million worth of their products to a small start-up that had no experience of operating in Brazil nor had a local leader up until then, let alone any employees! But stranger things have happened, and the team did pull it off by providing convincing arguments to Roche on the strength and experience of our team, our marketing plan to grow the sales, and the sheer entrepreneurial energy of moksha8. There was high-fiving, backslapping, and drunken late night partying all around after we signed the partnership. The rush of closing a deal for any team is amazing, but for an entrepreneurial team to close the very first landmark transaction that kick-started their company is a feeling that is hard to explain. For in those moments, all the hard work, late nights, the sacrifices of being away from family, seems worthwhile. The vision and dream of taking this start-up to conquer the world and to create an innovative disruption was now becoming a reality. Sure, there was a whole lot of hard work ahead in executing on all the plans for the product launch, taking market share from competitors, doing more deals, growing the organization, and hiring people. But in that moment of joy all these organizational and operational aspects became a matter of *when* rather than *if*. Until then, it's all an *if*, even though in the adrenaline-fueled, almost delusional start-up world, such doubts are hardly ever expressed in the open.

## Recepta: Comercio ou Inovar

Brazil's pharmaceutical market is one of the more balanced within the BRIC (Brazil, Russia, India, China) countries; in fact probably across all emerging markets. Brazil has both a strong local generics industry as well as original patented drugs from multinationals that are often reimbursed by the government, unlike India which is a heavily generics-inclined market and mostly out-of-pocket. In contrast, China does not have as strong a local generics industry due to perceived and sometimes real lack of quality despite a low re-imbursement from the government. Similarly in Russia, though there is adequate re-imbursement from the government at least for expensive medicines, there is a lack of a strong local generics industry due to quality concerns like in China. Over the last decade, if you were to look at the top 10 companies in the private market segment of each country and compare the distribution of local vs. multinational companies, India will be characterized by predominantly local companies (90%); China and Russia predominantly multinational (80-90%); and only Brazil would have represented a more balanced split of 50-50.

The uniqueness of the Brazilian pharmaceutical market extends to beyond just a balanced market presence of local generics versus that of patented drugs. For such a large geography, the distribution networks in Brazil are fairly well established and concentrated as compared to other big markets such as China, Russia, and India. Major distributors and pharmacy chains – BR Farma, Drogaria, Profarma, RaiaDrogasil, among others – dominate the market. Given the tropical climate and the vast territory of Brazil, there is also an extra requirement for manufacturers to establish the stringent temperature and humidity stability testing for products (known as Zone 4 stability tests). Another unique feature of the market is the diagnostic centres, with regional players dominating the sector. In contrast to many other countries, the diagnostics test results in Brazil can only be shared with the patient who then has the freedom to approach any doctor for analysis of the results and potential treatment options. This helps somewhat break-up what has become a nexus between hospitals, doctors, and diagnostics centres in several other countries.

The healthcare market in Brazil is also unique as compared to other emerging economies for one other reason. Under the law, every Brazilian citizen is provided the right to basic healthcare. In practice, more than 80% of the population has access to basic drugs covered by their national health insurance system called the Sistema Único de Saúde (SUS) or the Unified Health System. **In fact, such are the constitutional rights that irrespective of the price of the medicines or the cost of medical procedures, every single Brazilian can demand the best available care for their needs.** In pretty much every case where Brazilian patients have sued the government in court, they have won and forced the state to pay for their health needs. Many companies have capitalized on this unique aspect of Brazil's healthcare system, working closely with patient advocacy groups in raising the profile for certain diseases and involving the government in the healthcare needs of patients.

Genzyme (now part of Sanofi Group) is a leading example of a company that has positioned itself strongly in Brazil. Genzyme manufactures drugs for rare genetic diseases such as Gaucher's and Fabry's Disease, and Genzyme drugs for these diseases often cost tens of thousands of dollars per patient per year. After the US and Western Europe, Brazil ranks the highest globally in terms of revenues generated for Genzyme products primarily due to the company's efforts in working closely with patient groups and government to provide access to its drugs.

Despite a relatively progressive state-industry partnership and reimbursement policy, the life science innovation in Brazil, however, is still at a nascent stage. Brazil very much falls into the *State Innovator* cluster, and many of the VITAL framework elements are missing. In my view, of all the emerging markets, Brazil should be leading in innovation since many of the macro level dynamics are strong. The government reimburses most of the novel and expensive medicines, providing strong incentives for innovative products (L of VITAL), and patent protection is one of the highest within emerging markets. Brazil's healthcare regulatory body, ANVISA, has aligned its clinical trials and approvals framework closely with that of the US FDA. Further, the government is trying to implement several initiatives and has allocated robust funding to build biotech clusters in Rio de Janeiro and Sao Paulo, though this is still in its early days. The universities and research institutions have a strong base with leading academic centres such as the University of Sao Paulo, and the Fiocruz and INCA (National Cancer Institute of Brazil) in Rio (A of VITAL). Finally there is high-quality talent, which is being nurtured with generous grants and training programs such as 'Science Without Borders' from the government to leverage these strong macro factors.

Despite all these seemingly favourable enablers, one struggles to understand the cause for this nascent stage of life science innovation in Brazil. To understand this, let us scratch the surface a little.

Although the A and L of VITAL are strong, there are few other elements missing. The academic research is not translating into either high-quality publications in leading journals or a significant uptick in life sciences patents from Brazil. There remains a lack of robust funding (V of VITAL) for early discoveries both in the academic centres as well as for start-ups that may want to translate such research into products. The R&D infrastructure (I of VITAL) is still evolving, further impeding the translation of such discoveries into the clinic and the marketplace. There is another factor at play here – in some ways, unique to Brazil. Much of the government funding is going into *"technology transfer"* – getting access to technology platforms from the US and Europe, in exchange for capital and opening of the domestic market to the Western companies. And this is where I feel Brazil is missing the opportunity. Given the immense successes of *trading* its natural resources over the years to build a high performing economy, Brazil is trying to replicate the same policies in life sciences by *trading in* assets and technologies for local industry development rather than putting in place an ecosystem that can *create* such innovation on its home turf. Russia is another such example of a country following this roadmap. Such a strategy works best in expansionary economic cycles, when natural resource prices remain high yielding a trade surplus, but runs into trouble when prices are low. Unless the resources can be channelled towards a *create* strategy, Brazil risks getting into a status quo where it will continue to seek innovation from abroad and try to adapt it to the local environment in exchange for its capital resources.

This is not to say that there are no innovative companies in Brazil. One such example is Recepta Biopharma based in Sao Paulo that has built a strong pipeline of cancer treatments currently in clinical testing. It boasts of a unique model whereby Recepta has built strong scientific partnership with the Ludwig Centre in New York. It performs most of the research work through a network of labs across Brazil at the University of Sao Paulo and Butantan Institute amongst others, and has skilfully tapped into local capital and state funding. Founded in 2005, the company now has several biological molecules for cancers currently being tested in clinic. But Brazil needs to foster an environment and ecosystem that can facilitate many more such Receptas before it can unlock the country's full innovation potential.

## What's Next for Brazil?

I envision that the government's desire to diversify from a natural resources-focused economy into a high-tech and innovation-driven one bodes well for biomedical research and will help Brazil make significant advances in the coming years. Brazil has some of the key VITAL elements in place such as strong academic centres (A) and government policies (L) that reward innovation. The vast talent pool and entrepreneurial spirit in Brazil is an added advantage. However, it needs to provide stronger funding for its research centres, create mechanisms that can help translate academic research into start-up ventures, and to build R&D infrastructure around its key academic and biotech clusters. There is also tremendous opportunity to tap into the large biodiversity in Brazil to create an innovative industry in nutraceuticals, for example. Above all, government investment policies need to shift away from the philosophy of *trading* assets into a cohesive strategy of *creating* assets. Only then can Brazil transition from a *State Innovator* into a *Future Innovator*.

Teotihuacan, Mexico

# Beetles and Teotihuacan

There is a common joke in Mexico about Aspirin being the best contraceptive – women use it by squeezing the pill between their knees! Brazil and Mexico are both Catholic nations, but if Brazil has a liberal, sex-on-the-beach kind of openness to it, Mexico is as conservative as you can possibly get in the South American continent.

After the successful launch of moksha8 in Brazil, our team identified Mexico as the ideal next destination given attractive local market dynamics. This expansion of our operations then brought me to Mexico where I spent good part of a year during 2008-09. Soon after finalizing a deal with Roche worth almost $150 Million in product revenues, we opened our Mexico City offices in early 2009. It took the team only three months to kick-start the operations after signing the deal with Roche, and we hired about 100 employees for the Mexican organization by the spring of 2009. The learning from launching our Brazil operations a year back was quickly and efficiently applied in Mexico.

One of my lasting memories from Mexico is during the month of December 2008 when the flu epidemic had just hit the globe. It was an eerie feeling; the streets of Mexico City were completely empty. The city, one of the largest in the world with an estimated 25 Million inhabitants, is always buzzing with energy and chaos but was deserted during these few days. I had never felt like this, until later in my life during the Chinese New Year period in Shanghai when streets do feel abandoned. It reminded me of the very first scene from the science fiction thriller *Vanilla Sky* when Tom Cruise walks out of his apartment building in New York City out to empty streets in Manhattan. Akram Bouchenaki, a good friend and colleague at moksha8, and I were stuck in Mexico City during the peak of the flu epidemic and could not get out to any international destination due to flight restrictions. So we decided to head out to Puerto Vallarta, a Mexican beach resort, for the weekend. There are direct flights between most of California's cities and Puerto Vallarta, and there were large numbers of American tourists on the beaches. From empty Mexico City streets in the morning, we were at an exclusive beach resort crowded with mostly Americans by the afternoon, all during an epidemic; the irony wasn't fully lost on us. Coincidently, we were in the middle of in-licensing a flu product from Biocryst, a company in San Francisco, during this time. The deal was subsequently signed in 2009 and the product, Peramavir, was launched in Mexico in 2010 to help patients in the event of such epidemics.

## *Salud!*

Mexico is a country mired in corruption, unfortunately, similar to India. One of the most striking features of the economy and business are the monopolies, almost non-existent in any other economies the size of Mexico. For all practical purposes, there's only one company in telecom (Movil) that owns roughly 90% of the market share, in the process making its owner one of the richest men in the world; cement (Cemex); oil and gas (Pemex); and so forth. The only sector where there is true diversification and capitalist market forces competing is, sadly, the narcotics business – multiple cartels fighting, often brutally, to gain a slice of a very lucrative market.

The healthcare sector also mirrors, at least in certain sub-segments, the broader Mexican landscape. Take, for example, the distributors. There are three main distributors that control about 80% of the market – Casa Saba, Mazem, and Nadro. Now, on the surface this is a healthy competition similar to the US where McKesson, AmeriHealth, and Cardinal are three main distributors and competitors. However, once you scratch the surface you quickly figure out that the same family owns two of the three distributors in Mexico, *and* a close relative of the same family owns the third (I should add that this is anecdotal information from local sources, and in 2011 the US distributor McKesson acquired a majority equity stake in Mazem). This would then explain why Mexico has historically one of the highest pharmaceuticals distributor margins in the world, to the tune of 15-25%, and sometimes higher, versus low single digit margins in most other markets globally. There are, of course, multiple other factors playing into this equation, but the fact that the pharmaceutical distribution sector might be a pseudo-monopoly is probably one of the forces driving this dynamic.

Mexico's pharmaceutical market, however, mirrors Russia and China more than India or Brazil. There are very few good local Mexican companies, with the multinationals largely dominating the self-pay, private market segment; the government-paid sector does have predominance of local companies due to drug pricing and protectionist policies. Part of this dynamic can be explained by the prevalence of low-quality medicines from the local Mexican pharmaceutical players versus the high-quality ones from multinationals, which often becomes a barrier for local players in capturing market share. It is a market dynamic similar to Russia and China. In contrast, Brazil and India have several local companies with strong quality credentials and brands, competing with the multinationals.

Similar to India, Mexico is largely out-of-pocket although there are several government schemes that help certain sections of the society access medicines and hospital emergencies affordably. Given the out-of-pocket dynamics, it also results in the market being highly price sensitive. However, unlike India, where the prices of medicines are largely low across the board, the Mexico market is fairly segmented with differential pricing. This is largely due to the fact that whereas in India there are a lot of local companies with high brand recognition and quality that patients trust, in Mexico, the consumers still prefer multinational brands, which have a strong quality perception even if the price is higher. So while India is a volume-driven market, Mexico is still largely a price-driven market – for a population of roughly 120 Million, Mexico's pharmaceutical market was valued at $15 Billion in 2013, compared to the Indian market of a similar size of $15 Billion for a population that is 11 times larger than that of Mexico.

Mexico also happens to be one of the richest countries in Latin America, with a GDP (purchasing power parity) per capita of $16,500 as per World Bank figures for 2013, higher than Brazil's $15,000. This wealth is, however, very unevenly distributed and Mexico would rank alongside Russia and India as the other countries with such vast income disparity. There are several public health programs to improve access for the poorer sections of the society such as the Seguro Popular, which is a national low-cost health insurance program, and the national social security system, IMSS, but these too have not been successful in broadening healthcare coverage and access across the country. The more affluent centres such as Mexico City have much better access, hospital infrastructure, and doctor-patient ratio than the poorer parts of Mexico, making the provision of a universal quality healthcare a significant challenge for the government. This was a market insight that was judiciously recognized and captured by Farmacia Similares.

## Same as Innovator, Just Cheaper

An interesting case study, which further provides insights into the Mexican healthcare and business dynamics, is that of Farmacias Similares. This is a pharmacy chain started in Mexico by Mr. Victor Gonzalez Torres, nicknamed "Dr. Simi". These pharmacies are targeted at the low socio-economic sections of the population, selling generic medicines at a very low cost as compared to multinational branded drugs. Each of the pharmacies also has a doctor in-house who can provide diagnosis and prescribe medications for as low as 10-20 pesos (less than $2). In five years, the number of pharmacies of Farmacias Similares grew from scratch to over 30,000 across the country. Since the chain sold its own locally manufactured brands, it also gained almost a third of market share of total prescriptions in Mexico during this time. This is pretty much unprecedented anywhere in the world. How Farmacias Similares achieved this, reflects, in large part, on Mexico's business opportunities in the healthcare space.

If we apply the PIPET principle to Farmacias Similares, it was an overwhelming P – the business *Plan* – that worked exceptionally well. First, they could achieve a significant cost advantage since the generics launched by Farmacias used a loophole in the regulatory pathway to skip the clinical studies on bioequivalence. What this means is that unlike the generics worldwide who have to show that their drug is equivalent to the innovator-branded product, Farmacias did not have to. All they did was show that their product has the same active molecule, saving them the attendant costs for doing equivalence studies. Second, they launched a large scale and aggressive public campaign to market their products as "The same, only cheaper" – by some estimates, as much as 80% cheaper. In a price-sensitive market such as Mexico, this was an easy win. Third, they provided their customers with a one-stop-shop – a doctor to diagnose and prescribe medicines at a very low consultation cost and inexpensive medicines all under the same roof. This is significant for a nation with only about 2 doctors per 1,000 people, which is less than one-tenth of European levels and less than half of that in Southeast Asian countries. Finally, they overcame the access issue in a large country like Mexico by building these pharmacies in poor neighbourhoods within a small perimeter, so that patients didn't have to worry about traveling too far out from their homes for health needs. Of course, underlying all of these factors was an important element of politics and government machinery that was leveraged very well by Mr. Torres who understood those dynamics thoroughly.

Another local Mexican company, Genomma Labs, also leveraged some of these principles very well leading to its tremendous success. Their business model was equally simple – launch as many products as you can, as quickly as you can, in the most cost-effective way, and then be brutally disciplined at cutting back on the products that do not achieve profitability within a strict time frame. It also supplemented this strategy with an aggressive public campaign through various media channels, including a channel that was run by the owners of Genomma. In the over-the-counter (OTC), beauty products, and nutritional supplements segments, Genomma Labs was able to gain market share and build a strong franchise very quickly which it then leveraged to enter the more lucrative space of prescription medicines.

## Avenue of the Dead

All this is good but why, you may ask, have I titled this chapter Beetles and Teotihuacan? During the time I spent in Mexico, taxis were an adventure in themselves, not just because of the rather old models of these vehicles but also due to the turbulent times during 2008-2010. You had to be careful of which taxis to hire. The Beetles were my favourite and, as I was soon about to find out, the most dangerous. These Beetles did not have the front passenger seat. It was basically removed, apparently to make it easier for passengers to easily slide into the back seat of the car. However, anecdotally, this was done to make it easier for kidnappings and hold-ups, which were rampant in Mexico during those days. This was the period when drug wars were raging between cartels as well as one that saw a general spike in violent crime across Mexico.

And on my very first trip to Mexico City, my good friend and colleague Fred Gaume and I hired a Beetle taxi at 2am, after a good night out drinking in local bars. Neither of us knew much Spanish at that time, were both new to the country, and fairly tipsy. It was only next morning, when chatting with our Mexican colleagues, that we realized how close we came to experiencing the Mexican standoff! I guess I have always been fascinated by adventure, but this was pushing the limits a bit too far even by my own rather cavalier standards. I remember meeting a gentleman who was the general manager of a leading multinational company in Mexico City at the time and observing his wrists scarred with several marks (for confidentiality, I will not name the company or this individual). It was only when I got to know him well that I learned of the story behind those wrist marks. During his assignment to a South American nation (not Mexico), he was kidnapped along with two other colleagues for several months. They were kept handcuffed and tied to trees during this entire ordeal, while the multinational company and the government negotiated their release with the kidnappers! After that initial experiment with the Beetle taxis, I never hired those again and only relied on the Elite Taxis' services.

Teotihuacan was where I organized a team visit right after we had launched our Mexico office and closed on the major transaction with Roche. Teotihuacan is also known as the 'Pyramids of Mexico'. I figured it would be a good cultural immersion for the team. Located about 50 kilometres from Mexico City, the name literally translates into "Place of the Gods" since the Aztecs believed that the universe was created from this place. It is a beautiful view as you drive into this ancient 'city' and the site includes the Pyramid of the Sun and the Pyramid of the Moon. It is an exceptionally well-structured layout highlighting how the ancient settlements planned their cities. The Pyramid of the Sun is the largest in Teotihuacan, and the third largest pyramid in the world, with a height of almost 70 meters and roughly 2000 steps from the bottom to the top of the pyramid. The team took almost an hour walking up to the top (in 40 degrees Celsius heat!) We even competed with each other, in true moksha8 spirit, to be the first to reach the top. I believe Dee Athwal won the race but that was expected since Dee was probably the fittest of the lot. Once at the top, the tour guide told us the stories about Teotihuacan, how these platforms at the top of pyramids were used for human sacrifices, and the victims decapitated and their heads rolled down the stairs. No wonder the avenue that is flanked by the pyramids is aptly named the "Avenue of the Dead"! Not exactly the cultural immersion I wanted for the team, I'll tell you that. The history of Mexico, though, is underestimated globally, often overshadowed by the Indian, Chinese, or Egyptian civilizations.

## Avenue of Innovation

So how does modern science in Mexico compare to its rich history? Mexico is very much a hallmark of the *Path Seekers* cluster – unlike the Avenue of the Dead, the Avenue of Innovation is still trying to pave its way. Innovation in the life sciences, and in general, unfortunately has lagged miserably in this key emerging market and of all the countries discussed in this book Mexico (and Egypt) has the longest journey ahead to achieve innovation. In spite of the strong growth dynamic of the pharmaceutical market, the country has not been able to grow its scientific base or attract multinationals to do high-tech R&D or manufacturing as is the case, for example, in Singapore, China, or South Korea in Asia or to a certain extent in Brazil, its Latin American competitor. Pretty much all the aspects of the VITAL framework are missing in the case of Mexico. There is hardly any government or private funding available for cutting edge science (the V of VITAL), and the government has been behind the curve in providing strong policies and incentives to foster innovation (L of VITAL). Even the leading academic and research institutions such as UNAM and CINVESTAV are struggling to attract talent or funding, and there are only rare, isolated successes such as Carlos Slim financing the genomics institute INMEGEN. The talent pool is acutely missing and under-trained (T of VITAL), with little or no R&D infrastructure (I of VITAL) even in key cities of Monterrey and Mexico City. In addition to the fact that key VITAL factors are missing, another issue is that of centralized research capabilities with as much as 40% of national scientific activity concentrated in just Mexico City, leaving other parts of the vast country struggling to be scientifically competitive.

But Mexico has an opportunity to leapfrog many of its emerging markets peers and channel its resources into a world-class innovation hub, potentially in Mexico City.[16] It can learn from China on how to build bioclusters, from Israel about incubator programs and early-stage financing models, from South Korea about translational and clinical expertise, and from India, on ways to foster entrepreneurship (or at least how not to hinder it!)[17] Of course it has

---

[16]   Evolution of Chinese bioclusters as a framework for investment policies in emerging markets. Ajay Gautam. *Nature Reviews Drug Discovery.* Volume 14, 8, January 2015. The paper analyses 8 bioclusters in China using academic and entrepreneurial intensity, and proposes investment policies for other emerging markets bioclusters such as Tel Aviv, Seoul, Bangalore, and Singapore among others.

[17]   A framework for biomedical innovation in emerging markets. *Nature Reviews Drug Discovery.* Volume 13, 646-647, September 2014. Ajay Gautam and Steve Yang. The paper analyses 11 emerging markets – China, South Korea, Israel, India, Brazil, Russia, Singapore, Poland, South Africa, Mexico, and Turkey – and proposes a framework for biomedical innovation across these markets using funding levels and R&D ecosystems as key parameters.

better role models just north of its borders in San Diego or San Francisco or even Houston for life science hubs, but as aptly captured in *Why Nations Fail* [18] that might be too hard a model to emulate right off the bat. This "*south-south emulation*", as I call it, within the key emerging markets is an easier model to replicate, share, and learn from, as well as to partner with. A Chinese high-tech park such as Zhangjiang, which often operates as a real estate company, could be an ideal partner for Mexico in building a biotech complex, bringing along their experiences on designing and operating such a biocluster, as an example.

There are hardly any cases of truly innovative companies in Mexico pursuing cutting edge science. The one company that probably comes close is Probiomed. As is the case of many comparable companies across the emerging markets, Probiomed started as a small manufacturing operation for active pharmaceutical ingredients. Founded in the mid-1970s, it soon graduated to be a generics manufacturer and a key player in the Mexico pharmaceutical market by the late 1980s and early 90s. It was only in the mid-1990s, however, that its dynamic founder and CEO Jaime Uribe decided to steer the company towards innovative products, initially to build capabilities and expertise in the R&D space for biological drugs and vaccines. Jaime challenged the organization to be a true leader in innovation and forged collaborations with companies and institutions in US, Europe, and Israel. Probiomed was the first local company in Mexico to bring to market a locally developed drug for anaemia and cancer, with all technology developed at its labs in Mexico. It is today one of the true leaders in not only the Mexican market but has also built strong expertise to compete on a global scale. Unfortunately, such cases are few and Mexico needs many more such success stories to achieve its full innovation potential.

## What's Next for Mexico?

I envision that Mexico will continue to struggle over the coming years in its attempt to foster biomedical innovation, not due to lack of opportunities but rather due to the indifference of the government in formulating a cohesive strategy. Several of the VITAL elements are missing or non-existent. There

---

[18]    Why Nations Fail: The Origins of Power, Prosperity, and Poverty (2012). Daron Acemoglu and James A. Robinson. The book from a MIT economist and a Harvard political scientist provides insights into why nations develop differently, with some prospering and accumulating wealth while others fail.

needs to be stronger funding for academic centres, mechanisms to support entrepreneurs in creating life science start-ups, and incentives to pursue innovative ideas. The R&D infrastructure is lagging behind most emerging markets and severely impeding the translation of ideas from the labs into the clinic and commercial opportunities. There are no obvious biotech clusters for such a large economy. Mexico has also failed to tap into a resource that can have profound impact on local innovation – the large numbers of Mexican citizens in the US. There are minimal incentives for these individuals to go back to Mexico and create new companies or start their research labs at academic centres. In some ways, Mexico suffers from the proximity to the US. A Chinese, Indian, or Korean professional, for example, often longs to go back to their home country, be closer to family and friends, and have a meaningful impact on their country's local environment. In contrast, a Mexican professional is often just a short flight away from family and friends, and misses that connection a bit less than a Chinese or an Indian. However, governments in China and South Korea have created incentives for professionals – such as start-up funding, innovation ecosystems, R&D infrastructure, to name a few – to head back to their home country. Mexico has largely lagged behind in implementing any such incentives and unfortunately may continue to be an innovation *Path Seeker* for the foreseeable future.

A picture of Dubai Marina (handful of foreground buildings) and the Jumeirah Lake Towers (background buildings) separated by the Sheikh Zayed highway. During the recession of 2008 up until 2011, most of the Jumeirah Lake Tower apartments were empty – a total of 40-50 buildings consisting of thousands of apartments.

# The Arab Spring

The first thing you notice as you walk out of the Dubai airport is how hot it is, even for someone who grew up in India and spent significant time in Brazil and Mexico, not to mention Texas. The 'winter' temperature is around 18-20 degrees Celsius (north of 70 degrees Fahrenheit). Summers can be as high as 55 degrees Celsius! But you also notice how cool the city is – flashy architecture, sprawling malls, pristine beaches, exquisite hotels, state-of-the-art infrastructure, uber-fashion, and it even has a man-made ski range inside a shopping mall. The city was built only a few decades ago and is now a key hub and centre for global trade. The growth of Dubai from a desert city back in the 1970s to the glistening business mecca of today is owed to the futuristic plans of HH Sheikh Rashid Saeed al Makhtoum. The late ruler of Dubai epitomized the *"build it and they will come"* vision, subsequently taken to new heights by his son HH Sheikh Mohammed al Makhtoum.

I grew up in India, and had the chance to travel and live across the US, Brazil, and Mexico, and visit other parts of the world for work, before moving to Dubai. All the cities I had lived in, or travelled to, had a long history, a character, an identity that was defined over many decades and centuries. Dubai, in contrast, is a young city and dazzled me with its glitter – the Medinat Jumeirah resort is designed like Venice, with canals and gondola boat rides providing the backdrop to a 5-star luxury hotel. The fountains in front of the Burj Khalifa, the tallest building in the world, are designed after the Venetian Hotel in Las Vegas with similarly themed fountain shows every hour. Bur Dubai, the old town of Dubai, has ferries and boat rides that take you directly into the Spice Souk, the famous spice market. If you fancy some jewellery shopping there is the Gold Souk, a large complex in the Jumeirah neighbourhood. This may actually be familiar to many of the readers who have travelled to Dubai, but for me it was intriguing how a city with no history, almost with an artificiality about it – what I call a 'photo-shopped city' – can be a fascination for many people globally!

Shopping malls remain one of the biggest attractions for travellers to Dubai, and the Dubai Mall, the largest mall globally, has every brand under the sun that you can imagine. One such brand at the Dubai Mall is Patchi. My ignorance about Dubai extended to this chocolate brand as well, which now has extensive presence across the Middle East, Asia, and other parts of the world. And Patchi happens to be one of the most admired brands of chocolates, strong enough to compete with the likes of Godiva. Patchi is a brand based out of Saudi Arabia (or Lebanon, depending on who you ask). The shopping malls of Dubai, Beirut, Doha, Jeddah, Cairo, Istanbul, and other Middle East, North African, and Asian cities have Patchi shops where people can design and order their own chocolates. You can concoct a mixture of dates, dry fruits, and exotic white or dark chocolates to design your own personalized chocolates. Very few chocolate brands have the loyalty and diversity of Patchi. And that is what Dubai represents in my view – a patch work of exotic hotels, malls, neighbourhoods, beaches, restaurants, and nightclubs that you can mix and match at leisure to enjoy all that the city has to offer.

As part of building my start-up in the Middle East, I also spent a significant amount of time in Saudi Arabia, which is the largest market in the Gulf. If Dubai is all glitter and glamour, then Riyadh is as staid as it can get in the Gulf region. The high temperatures and dry desert weather is further stifling due to the social restrictions. As a single guy traveling to Saudi, I had to always be seated in the section of the restaurants that is reserved exclusively for men. Each of the public areas in Saudi is divided into areas based on gender and marital status. A woman can mostly be seated in areas for women or in the family section, irrespective of their marital status, but men not accompanied by a woman can largely only sit in the men-only section. Alcohol is prohibited, even in 5-star hotels. Women are clad strictly in hijabs in public places, and hardly any women drivers are seen on the road. You can imagine that the days I spent in Saudi were mostly focused on work and meetings, and I was always eager to get back to Dubai.

## Chaos Theory

In late 2009, I decided to trade the Brazilian samba and Mexican tequila for Middle Eastern belly dancing and *sheesha* (a tobacco smoking pipe, also known as *hookah*, popular among patrons at cafes and restaurants in the Middle East). Hocine Sidi-Said, a good friend and colleague from moksha8 and Pfizer days, and I decided to start Bio-nAbler, a healthcare investment firm based out of Dubai. The global recession was still very much roiling the markets but we felt the Middle East provided a compelling opportunity. During the peak of the Great Recession, Dubai had defaulted heavily on its debt and all indications were that the city was in the middle of a complete meltdown. Voila! As a stroke of genius or insanity (depending on your perspective), I felt that it was the ideal time to jump into this turmoil since things can only move up from this bottom. And it was probably partly inspired by what Warren Buffet has always said "Be fearful when everyone is greedy, and be very greedy when everyone is fearful". So I moved to Dubai, armed with little more than an enthusiasm to start something new and dreams of creating a business as successful, if not more, as we had done in Latin America. Little did Hocine and I realize the challenges we would face, trying to build our firm in the midst of the Great Recession and the Arab Spring that would soon spread like wildfire throughout the Middle East. We were joined in this adventure by Richard Kassaby, a finance whiz, and Amgad Botros, an expert in the hospital and healthcare services industry. Richard and Amgad are both Aussies of Egyptian descent and spent significant time with us in the Middle East helping build Bio-nAbler.

The cultural and business environment, and the healthcare industry, in the Middle East could not be more dramatically different than that of Latin America. First, the obvious: the sunny beaches of Rio with the sun-bathed, bikini-clad beauties are a far cry from the burkha-clad, ultra-conservative culture of Riyadh. The Ramadan month is also a unique experience. During the holy month, it is a social norm, and in some places strictly enforced, to not eat or drink in public during the day. A few restaurants do remain open but make it a point to cover the dining area with dark curtains so no one from outside can view the food or drinks, as a mark of respect for those who fast during that period. However, late evenings and nights are an entirely different atmosphere. Once the fast breaks in the evening, most places are open until 4 to 5 am the next morning with large crowds gathering with friends and family over food, drinks, and *sheesha*. This is where I also experienced a unique business meeting culture. During Ramadan, most meetings would happen after late evenings, mostly after 9 or 10 pm once the fast was broken. Many offices remained closed during the day or only operated during early mornings. People will often sleep from late morning through early evening just before fast-breaking time, and will then stay awake until wee hours of the next morning. During the three Ramadans I celebrated in the Middle East, many of our business meetings occurred after midnight!

## *Talent Gulf*

The pharmaceutical markets in the Gulf Cooperation Council (GCC; Gulf) countries – Saudi Arabia, UAE, Kuwait, Qatar, Bahrain, and Oman – are fairly well structured. From a regulatory, market access, insurance, and pricing perspective, these markets are modelled after the western ones. The prices of drugs are often comparable to the US or European prices. A product that is approved by the US FDA or the EU's EMEA faces few, if at all any, hurdles for approval and launch in these countries and in many cases does not even require any local clinical studies. The Gulf countries have also harmonized their systems so as to make it easy for other countries to approve the drugs if one of the countries approves it, although in practice, most Gulf countries always look to Saudi to take the lead on novel products. The government largely pays for healthcare needs of the local population, and there are several private health insurance options available for the large number of expats residing in the Gulf. There are state-of-the-art hospitals and clinics throughout the Gulf region, although the richer clientele still prefers to visit UK, Switzerland, France, or the US for their complicated medical needs. There are also an increasing number of patients from the Gulf visiting India, Singapore, Malaysia, or Thailand as part of medical tourism. Saudi remains the largest pharmaceutical market in the region, but comparatively is still a meagre $4 Billion in value versus its much larger emerging markets counterparts in Asia or Latin America.

Most of the products sold in the Gulf countries, irrespective of the industry, are imported. This includes clothes, dairy, juice, cars, medicines, cosmetics, and the list goes on. Talent is also something that is largely imported. Almost 70-80% of the UAE population is expats, and similar to the overall population dynamics in the UAE, nearly 80% of physicians are also expats. However, even in Saudi with a significantly lower proportion of overall expat population, there is a very high proportion of expat doctors. Many are from the US, Europe, and India, but a significant proportion is also from Jordan and Egypt, the two nations within the Middle Eastern region with good medical schools, pharmacy programs, and a large number of graduates. Similar dynamics plays out in other industries as well, with a majority of employees being expats. Such skewed work force dynamics has led Saudi Arabia to launch its 'Saudization' program: businesses are required to hire a fixed quota of local Saudi employees, and the government provides incentive programs for both employers and employees including educational and skills training for the local population. This was also an additional tool the Saudi monarchy used skilfully to protect itself from the Arab Spring.

Another key gap in the Middle East and North Africa (MENA) region is professional management. It is a region where business is run heavily on relationships and networks, more so in the healthcare industry where the government is the primary customer. There are significant efficiencies to be extracted from operations across the spectrum of regional pharmaceutical companies, and MENA has largely been off the radar for most US or European biotech companies that are focused on entering the larger markets in Asia, Latin America, or Russia. This was, in a nutshell, the genesis of Bio-nAbler – on the one hand, to bring a hands-on operational expertise along with capital investments to the MENA regional companies and, on the other, an opportunity for the US, European, and Asian companies to partner with Bio-nAbler to enter the MENA markets. In some ways, Bio-nAbler was a combination of Momentum BioVenture's investment thesis from Houston and moksha8's premise to build a commercial platform in Latin America.

## Across the Indian Ocean

One of our Board members at Bio-nAbler was Dr. B.R. Shetty, a larger-than-life figure and one of the leading Indian business tycoons in UAE and the Middle East. BR, as he is fondly and respectfully called by his close associates, built the NMC Group to one of the most successful and largest healthcare conglomerates in the UAE. He literally built NMC from scratch over the 35 years of his life in the Emirates. A pharmacist by training and married to a doctor, he moved to Abu Dhabi in the early 1970s with a few hundred dollars in his pocket. He started by establishing a healthcare services business in the UAE and over the next three decades built an empire worth billions of dollars, spanning across pharmaceuticals manufacturing, hospitals, and healthcare clinics in UAE and Egypt, educational institutions across the UAE, and the UAE Exchange which is one of the largest money remittance platforms for the Middle East and India. His rags-to-riches story has been an inspiration to a generation of Indian immigrants and entrepreneurs in the Gulf countries.

Dr. Shetty's offices are often adorned with pictures of him standing next to HH Sheikh Makhtoum, the ruler of Dubai. During my first visit to his office, he proudly walked me through the various events where he had shared the stage with different royalty and luminaries in the Gulf. The glint in his 70 plus year-old eyes showed the pride of a man who started with a few dirhams in his pocket and rose by his sheer hard work and ingenuity to stand next to highly respected individuals. I still distinctly remember the first board meeting of our company when I met BR. I had just moved to Dubai, was finding my feet and settling into a new city, and BR made it a point to make me feel at home. Maybe he saw a young man coming in to this land with the same dreams he himself had over three decades back, or maybe it was just his magnanimity. This was just one of the many aspects of BR that made him such a successful businessman: his ability to connect with people.

Another part was a deep desire to serve his community. His entire conglomerate – clinics, hospitals, educational institutions, money remittance – were tailored to the immigrants from the Indian subcontinent. BR realized very early on, he recounted to me, just as the late HH Sheikh Rashid Saeed Al Makhtoum, that the Indian subcontinent's population would both be a large portion of immigrants as well as the largest contributor to building the economy and prosperity of the Emirates. He judiciously priced such offerings so as to provide cost-effective hospitals to middle class immigrants from India, schools for their kids, an exchange platform for them to send money home to their parents and families, and even hired mostly Indians in his enterprises. The brand loyalty of his businesses, such as NMC and UAE Exchange, is unparalleled, in spite of challenges from competitors and the occasional quality issues.

A vastly different and more recent success story I love to share is that of Omar Khan, an entrepreneur who moved to Dubai after leaving his comfortable job with Boehringer Ingelheim in the UK. Omar founded Dayarn Pharma, a pharmaceutical sales force outsourcing company, based out of Dubai. Omar basically wanted to start a moksha8 for the Gulf region, and approached us, Hocine and me, for advice on partnering and potential investment from BionAbler. Having been through the experience in Latin America on a similar business model, and wary of the challenges that such a model would face in the Gulf, we steered Omar to what we thought would be the best possible way to capture the opportunity. Incidentally, I, more than Hocine, personally thought that the opportunity would be a tough one to crack and did advise Omar and his team to look into alternative, more profitable options such as acquiring a product portfolio or business. Thankfully, he ignored my advice. With his sharp focus and determination, Omar kept at his vision of building a niche sales force based model for the pharmaceutical clients. I was pleasantly surprised when he was able to not only bring in business from the likes of global pharmaceutical players such as GSK and Boehringer, but also strike a strategic partnership with Quintiles, a leading global pharmaceutical services organization, about 3-4 years after starting Dayarn. Kudos to his entrepreneurial spirit! You get to see the likes of Omar on a regular basis in the Gulf, a region with a rich entrepreneurial history.

## Black Gold, Cursed

One of the areas where the Gulf nations have lagged severely behind the Asian, Russian, and Latin American counterparts is in innovation; more so in life sciences. The Middle East lacks an innovation ecosystem, a city like Bangalore, Singapore, Shanghai, Sao Paulo, or St Petersburg that can boast of, or even aspire to, integrate the various VITAL elements.[19] Dubai has attempted to achieve this over the years starting with the economic zones it created for various sectors such as the Dubai Healthcare City (where Bio-nAbler as well as many other pharmaceutical companies were based); Dubai Internet City for IT/Software; or the Dubai Media City for Media/Communications. However, most of these zones soon became centres for *trading*, rather than *creating* true innovation where companies set up R&D units, discover innovative products, or develop local talent. Unlike a Bangalore or Shanghai, where several of the ingredients of the innovation ecosystem and VITAL framework were present, Dubai lacked a true focus on innovation. It did have a huge appetite and availability of government funding, a decent R&D infrastructure and strong government incentives (the V, I and L of VITAL), but lacked strong talent pool and leading universities and academia – the T and A of the VITAL cog. Although the city planned to emulate Singapore in this regard, there is no institution with the credibility of a National University of Singapore in Dubai,

---

[19]   Evolution of Chinese bioclusters as a framework for investment policies in emerging markets. Ajay Gautam. *Nature Reviews Drug Discovery*. Volume 14, 8, January 2015. The paper analyses 8 bioclusters in China using academic and entrepreneurial intensity, and proposes investment policies for other emerging markets bioclusters such as Tel Aviv, Seoul, Bangalore, and Singapore among others.

there are limited industry-academia partnerships, and minimal investments in high-tech R&D or manufacturing in contrast to Singapore.

Saudi Arabia has earlier this decade initiated an effort to create an innovation ecosystem with a $10 Billion (yes, that's a B!) endowment for the King Abdullah University of Science and Technology (KAUST) located in Thuwal, a small town close to Jeddah. In contrast to Dubai that does not have a leading academic centre, KAUST has a sprawling campus with international faculty and labs pursuing leading science, students from across the globe, and generous grants for post-doctoral fellows. Saudi with its KAUST and similar initiatives is hoping to have much more success than Dubai in creating a true innovation hub in the Gulf region. There are healthy signs that it is pursuing the right strategy, but it is still very early days.[20] A significant challenge for KAUST is to attract leading scientists and post-doctoral fellows to pursue science in a largely isolated region with respect to innovation. So although there are a number of joint appointments of professors from western universities, building a critical mass of talent in Jeddah is still at a nascent stage.

Nevertheless, the ambitious initiative of creating an innovation hub in Saudi with an impressive endowment for a new university and research campus was rightfully centred close to Jeddah, a city on the Red Sea that is infinitely more vibrant and liberal as compared to Riyadh (though still very conservative as compared to Dubai). Come to think of it, there is always something about cities on coasts that lends them a cache and creative vibe – Shanghai, Mumbai, Rio, Dubai, Istanbul, St. Petersburg – that is often not matched by their in-land counterparts – Beijing, Delhi, Sao Paulo, Riyadh, Moscow, Mexico City. One reason is that the cities on coasts were historical trading ports that were the first to see trade, immigrants, and new ideas coming into the country, making these cities an ideal playing field for novel experiments and lending them a chic edge. In contrast, the inland cities are mostly political capitals that are often sprawling with politicians, bureaucrats, and the like, and that heavy pall seeps into the psyche of these cities.

One of the reasons for the lack of innovation in the Gulf is often also attributed to historical business focus. The Gulf countries, as the saying goes, are both blessed and cursed – with *black gold*. Given the rich natural resources in oil and gas, the business elements have naturally been strong towards *trading* these assets, rather than *creating* technologies. In contrast, for example,

---

[20]    Same as footnote 19.

Singapore, South Korea, and Israel lacked such natural resources, and hence had to take the route of *creating* both an ecosystem and assets that were focused on innovation. It is this fundamental shift from *trading* to *creating* that is so urgently needed in the Gulf if the countries harbour a desire for biomedical innovation.

## Can the Mummies Return?

Egypt, of course, is very different from the Gulf nations. The pharmaceutical industry in Egypt is similar to Mexico, with the private market mostly dominated by multinationals due to quality concerns of the local manufacturers. However, the drug pricing in Egypt is closer to an Indian market than to Mexico, which makes it one of the more intriguing and difficult markets to operate in. For a population of 80 Million, the entire pharmaceutical market is valued at less than $4 Billion versus $15 Billion in Mexico for a population of 120 Million. Egypt is also largely an out-of-pocket market with the government paying very little of the healthcare burden and a low penetration of healthcare insurance, similar to Mexico and India. The healthcare infrastructure and access is comparatively well distributed, though, with almost 95% of Egyptians able to access primary healthcare within five kilometres of their homes.

Sigma Pharmaceuticals, based in Cairo, is one of the companies in which Eastgate Capital Group, a partner firm of Bio-nAbler, had invested. Hocine and I served as advisors for the growth strategy of Sigma. When I first met the management team at Sigma, what struck me about the company were the parallels with Genomma Labs from Mexico – broad diversified business, large portfolio of products, a media channel as part of the conglomerate to support direct-to-consumer marketing, and a similar philosophy banking on the large and growing consumer market, albeit much smaller in Egypt than in Mexico. One of the masterstrokes of Sigma was to identify a key niche in the Egyptian market – obesity, incidentally, also similar to Mexico. It launched a generic version of Xenical (orlistat), an innovator product from Roche, which is a drug for obesity and weight loss. Sigma's orlistat version turned out to be a massive commercial success in the Egyptian market, propelled by advertising through the company's media channels as well as retail marketing in shopping malls. This drove Sigma's strong revenue growth, positioning it as one of the leading local companies in Egypt.

Interestingly, as a parallel although for a very different reason, the other big market for Xenical globally at that time was Brazil where everyone wanted to lose weight quickly for the summers at the beach! While cosmeceuticals popularity in Brazil is easily explained by the beauty consciousness of Brazilian women, an intriguing and fascinating fact not very well known is that one of the highest per capita spending on cosmetics and beauty products globally is in Saudi Arabia. An often asked question – 'why is it so high when women wear *hijabs* in public'. It is a complex, cultural question. The answer I usually got when I asked this question to locals was that most Middle Eastern women love to pamper themselves at the spas – one such public luxury they get to enjoy.

PharmaAccess is another fascinating case study from Egypt and the Middle Eastern region. Khalid Amin founded the company to launch high-quality generics in Egypt, Lebanon, and the Gulf countries. An energetic cigar and football-loving young man from Cairo, he was also the CEO of a Dubai-based trading firm that did substantial business in Iran in parallel to running PharmaAccess from Cairo and Dubai. Here's how Khalid's week used to look like: he would leave Dubai on Sunday morning for Tehran, spend 2-3 days there, then return to Dubai for a couple of days, and on Thursday evening fly to Cairo for the weekend to spend time with his family, and return to Dubai on Saturday night (most of Middle East has working days from Sunday-Thursday with Friday and Saturday as the weekend). Repeat. Every week. Every month. All year round. And he was building two companies in parallel. I was in awe of this guy, amazed by his energy, focus, drive, and passion. And he did an excellent job at both firms. The trading firm grew to become one of the largest distributors in Iran during his tenure. PharmaAccess partnered with Acino, a European pharmaceutical company, to launch the first generic version of clopidogrel (a blood thinner medication) in UAE and Lebanon. In the middle of all this, he always found time to watch various football matches, whether it was the World Cup, European Cup, or any of the European Club Leagues with Barcelona and Spain being his favourite teams. A truly inspiring entrepreneur!

During my stay in Egypt, I would often discuss the innovation potential of Egypt with friends, colleagues, and business partners. The consensus was that, as is the case now several years later, Egypt's innovation landscape is fairly nascent. The strong generics industry and lack of incentives for innovative companies has resulted in hardly anything by way of a biotech ecosystem. The majority of local companies such as Sigma Pharma and Amoun Pharma are pursuing either generics or consumer products. The low prices further discourage industry to invest in lengthy and expensive R&D. Egypt's scientific and academic base is also weak, with only Cairo University as a key centre for research, and public research funding levels are one of the lowest for emerging markets. The vast talent pool is untapped with large numbers of clinicians, researchers, and pharmacists often migrating to the UAE or Saudi Arabia in search of better opportunities. In many ways, Egypt's and Mexico's ecosystems share similar challenges: both countries spend roughly 0.5% of GDP on research; if Mexico has the US as a neighbour that attracts the best minds from Mexico, many Egyptians migrate to Saudi Arabia for better opportunities; most of the research infrastructure is centralized in key cities such as Mexico City and Cairo, with rest of the country struggling to keep pace.

It is these challenges and opportunities within Egypt that inspired Ahmed Zewail to propose and champion the Zewail City of Science and Technology. Ahmed is an Egyptian-born Nobel laureate professor in chemistry at the California Institute of Technology. Similar to the KAUST in Saudi Arabia, the Zewail City of Science and Technology has been able to secure a large space just outside of Cairo to set up a $2 Billion ecosystem that would attract the best scientists from across the globe, reverse the brain drain from Egypt, and inspire young minds to pursue science at the city's centres of excellence. The presence of Ahmed Zewail helped attract several other Nobel laureates to the board of trustees that will direct the establishment of the city and implementation of the scientific projects. How successful is this initiative in reviving the scientific research in Egypt remains to be seen, but it is a significant step in the right direction.

## Hub and Spoke

Similar to some emerging markets, mono- or duopolies are a common phenomenon in the Middle Eastern countries. Take the case of the telecommunications industry in the UAE. There are basically two large companies, Etisalat and Du, both owned by the government that have complete duopoly of the market. An interesting way to divide the market within the two companies, something that I found fascinating and unique as compared to many other markets, is to divide Dubai into zones with each of these zones served either by Du or Etisalat for landlines and cable connections. Now this is not completely unique; even blocks of Manhattan are divvied up between various telecom companies. But what was interesting in a country where social media is fairly restricted was that depending on the zone of Dubai and the telecom company, you could access certain platforms, Skype and Facebook being two such examples, much more easily. So if you lived in Dubai Marina and were Du's customer, Skype was not an issue even though in a commercial area such as around Sheikh Zayed Road only a few kilometres from Dubai Marina with Etisalat as the telecom provider, Skype access was restricted. None of the social platforms would be easily accessible in most other areas such as Karama or Bur Dubai. There were always theories such as government clampdown on free speech and flow of information to justify this, but the local perspective was that it all came down to economics. None of the telecoms wanted a high immigrant population to use free services like Skype to call their home countries and cut out their profits. A more cynical local view was that the 'haves' always get more, and the 'have-nots' lose out – the upscale Dubai Marina where access was largely unrestricted had richer economic strata, whereas other localities were middle class or poor immigrants mostly from the Indian subcontinent. Irrespective of the theories, this strong government backing and high cash flows from a captive market allowed both Du and Etisalat to expand into the other Middle East and Africa markets in a big way, establishing both firms as the leading telecom players on the African continent, for example.

This focus and desire to build strong global players also led to the founding and growth of one of the most successful companies from Dubai, the flagship Emirates Airlines. It is not common knowledge that Dubai has literally zero oil – most of the oil resources in UAE are in Abu Dhabi and Sharjah. Which makes the growth of Dubai even more impressive. HH Sheikh Makhtoum realized early on in his *"build it and they will come"* vision that Dubai has an enviable geographical location. It is within a few hours flight from Europe, Central and East Asia, Russia, Africa, and the Indian subcontinent, as well as not being too far away from the Americas. The seeds of Dubai's dynamic growth over the decades were sown with the idea of establishing the city as the undisputable air traffic hub of the world. In the 1990s, the Dubai airport did not even rank in the top 20 busy airports of the world. Today, it is by far numero uno! And the Emirates Airlines is not only one of the finest airlines globally, it is also the rare one to survive industry downturns over the years while continuing to deliver strong profits. This is in spite of strong competition locally from Abu Dhabi's flagship Etihad, Istanbul's Turkish Airlines, and Doha's Qatar Airlines, all high-quality carriers. Such connectivity has also allowed Dubai to establish itself as the global hot spot for tourism, shopping, and hospitality sectors, and this *hub and spoke* strategy has helped created strong local players across multiple industries.

## Black Swan, not Black Gold Curse

But this was also the region where I experienced first-hand the political upheaval of the Arab Spring and how it impacted businesses across industries. I remember well the trip to Egypt just prior to the outbreak of the revolts against the Hosni Mubarak regime. The Four Seasons hotel on the Nile River is one of the oldest hotels in Cairo with breath-taking views of the river and of the Pyramids of Giza on a clear day. Just as the revolt and the ensuing violence broke out in Cairo, starting from the Tahrir Square in the city and quickly spreading across Egypt, the Four Season hotel was turned into a fortress, as was the case with other hotels across Cairo. Gone were the breath-taking views of the Nile River; all you could hear were the gunshots on the streets and see the smoke from the fires across the city. Many of my friends were worried about their families in Egypt, the anger and frustrations of the youth knew no targets and everything was fair game in their protests, something I delve into further in the last chapter discussing the socio-politico-economic aspects of such revolutions.

Just as an aside, it is intriguing that many of the centres where large scale protests broke out have the names starting with T: Tianamen Square in Beijing, Tahrir Square in Cairo, Taksim Square in Istanbul, to name a few.

The Arab Spring also directly impacted Bio-nAbler business. If the Great Recession had an indirect effect on my previous company moksha8 due to constrained financing and strategic shift, the Arab Spring was much more immediate and stark for my new one. Businesses in Egypt, Algeria, Bahrain, and Tunisia saw significant slowdowns. Our travel outside of UAE for several months was restricted to pretty much Saudi Arabia and Jordan. New investment dollar flows fell dramatically. We tried to adapt the business by focusing more on Turkey where many of our private equity and sovereign wealth fund partners were increasingly more comfortable to invest. But Turkey was not one of our key focus markets to start with; besides, it would take time and resources to build a portfolio of investments in a market that was now suddenly hot due to increased competition from many players. There is no way to plan for a

*Black Swan²¹* event such as the Arab Spring, but in hindsight Hocine and I were probably invested too heavily in the Gulf and North Africa countries and didn't balance out our geographical footprint by spreading our resources into India and Turkey, for example. As our projects and investments in Egypt, Algeria, and Iran, and even in Saudi and UAE, started to look volatile, we scrambled to raise fresh capital in parallel to focusing more on India and Turkey. The P – *Place* – of the PIPET, which was potentially attractive when we founded Bio-nAbler soon turned to be its most challenging aspect. We couldn't adapt our business quickly enough to a dramatically changed environment and eventually negotiated an investment into Bio-nAbler from the Eastgate Capital Group that helped the company survive through the turbulence.

Another sector impacted by the Arab Spring was real estate in Dubai, surprisingly in a positive way. Dubai's real estate took a major hit during the 2008 financial crises, with apartment prices falling as much as 50% in some neighbourhoods and even high-end properties in posh areas such as Marina and Downtown falling by as much as 25-30%. Localities such as Jumeirah Lake Towers had around 40-50 buildings, each 30-40 floors, all largely empty. A lot of people lost significant capital during the crises. But one of the outcomes of the Arab Spring in 2010 was a steady stream of cash flowing back into Dubai real estate. Interesting paradox, you may wonder! But dig deeper, and the dynamic becomes clearer. As Egypt, Syria, Libya, Algeria, Bahrain, and even Morocco to some extent, were being engulfed in the revolutions of the Arab Spring, the only safe haven was UAE, a cocoon of calm and stability in the middle of chaos. Wealthy Egyptians, Syrians, Libyans, Algerians, Tunisians, among others were pouring money into the Dubai real estate, relocating their families to Dubai to escape the violence and instability of their countries in search of better lives for their families. The school enrolments in major institutions such as GEMS, the largest school network in UAE and Middle East, had record new enrolments in the 2010-11 year during the height of the Arab Spring. Real estate prices today in Dubai are higher than the peaks just before the economic recession of 2008. As Warren Buffet once famously said, "Be greedy when people are fearful" worked out very well for the risk-seeking investors in the real estate sector if one invested in the early part of this decade.

---

21   The Black Swan: The Impact of the Highly Improbable (2007). Nassim Nicholas Taleb. The book analyses the impact of 'outlier' events, those rare and unpredictable occurrences, and how to build resilience against such events.

## What's Next for the Middle East?

I believe that the Middle Eastern countries have a significant challenge in creating viable innovation clusters. However, their challenge is unlike many other emerging markets. Most emerging economies are struggling with funding, R&D infrastructure or cohesive policies (V, I and L of VITAL). The Middle East – especially countries such as UAE and Saudi Arabia – has these aspects reasonably well covered. Their challenge is around strong academic institutions and talent (the A and T of VITAL). There are meaningful efforts in place to enhance the quality of research such as the ones at KAUST in Saudi Arabia, but these are still in very early stages. The Gulf countries will continue to be *Path Seekers* until they build strong academic and medical centres locally.

Egypt, in contrast, has almost all of the VITAL elements missing and is far behind its emerging markets peers in biomedical innovation. There is minimal start-up activity in the life sciences sector, scarce funding, limited R&D infrastructure, and almost complete lack of government initiative. One aspect that is relatively strong for Egypt, as compared to other Middle Eastern nations, is the talent pool and, with the right policies and investments, this resource can be tapped to foster innovation and start-up activity. The launch of the Zewail City is a good start in this direction. However, of all the countries covered in this book, Egypt has the longest road ahead in developing an innovation ecosystem and will continue to be a *Path Seeker* for the foreseeable future.

A picture of the frozen Moskva River during the month of February. With temperatures as low as 40 degrees centigrade below zero in Moscow, the frozen river looks identical to the adjoining road.

# Vodka, Caviar and Silicon Valley

I spent the last few years visiting and spending several days to weeks per quarter in Russia, primarily in Moscow and St Petersburg, as part of my role leading Asia Pacific and emerging markets scientific partnering at AstraZeneca. Of all the countries I have lived and worked in, Russia is definitely one of the most fascinating (and, of course, the coldest!) The challenges and the volatility of this market are matched only by the unparalleled optimism and passion of the Russian people. Every time I visit Russia, I am also reminded of Chanakya, the great Indian philosopher and scholar who once said "the most powerful weapon in the world is a woman's beauty and youth". And, other than Brazil, this country happens to be one place in the world where Chanakya must have definitely visited before penning those words.

The 'white nights' in St Petersburg during the summer months are another thing to savour. You can see people out on the streets as late as 2 am. The sun is still out well after 11 pm with people walking around in sunglasses, a fascinating sight. On one of my trips to St Petersburg, I visited the Russian Vodka Museum, where you can get a tour through the history of vodka over the past century in Soviet Union and post-Soviet Russia. The guided tour is a journey to discover the secrets of making vodka, drinking traditions, and a review of the different equipment used in the old days to make this staple Russian drink. It's an absolutely enchanting experience and you top off the tour with a sampling of six different vodkas served with caviar and traditional Russian appetizers. What struck me during the tour though is how Russia completely lost the plot in global vodka brands. Of all the major global brands – Belvedere from Poland, Grey Goose from France, Van Gogh (Netherlands), Absolut (Sweden), Skyy (US) – only Stolichnaya and Smirnoff are from Russia (and even Sminorff is now owned by Diageo, a UK company)! It is like Mexico losing the branding on Tequila or Scotland on Scotch.

## Russian Roulette

So how about Russian science and innovation? This is another area where the country, with such a rich history in science and technology, lost its historical edge on innovation and is now lagging behind global players. In fact, Russia has lost the edge on global branding in a number of industries – much like Vodka – and it is probably the only emerging market that does not have a truly global company. India has Tata, Infosys, and Reliance as global brands; China has Huawei, Lenovo, and Alibaba; Brazil has Embraer and Votorantim; Mexico has Movil; UAE has Emirates Airlines; South Korea has Samsung, Posco, and Hyundai; and so forth. This lack of strong local players in Russia has played out in the healthcare industry as well.

The Russian pharmaceutical market is one of the fastest growing across all emerging economies. This is driven by several factors – population dynamics, government initiatives such as the Pharma 2020 plan, recent introduction of the national drug insurance program, and increased focus from both multinational and local players. Russian patients and physicians are also immensely brand-focused, as is evident from the fact that of the top 10 pharmaceutical companies in Russia only one, Pharmstandard, is a local company. International brands are viewed as much higher quality than local players, and this is an area where the government is focused on improving quality standards for Russian companies. State-funded access programs for medicines form a significant part of the pharmaceutical sector, especially for the rare and expensive-to-treat diseases that are reimbursed by the government. Quality issues and infrastructure challenges, however, limit broad access and coverage. Most leading healthcare centres are concentrated in Moscow and St Petersburg, leaving vast population and geography of Russia without access to latest facilities. A large segment of the population is still not covered by any health insurance or reimbursement system. Hazardous lifestyles – almost 40% deaths in Russia are alcohol or tobacco-related – resulting in one of the lowest life expectancy globally is also a significant healthcare challenge.

One of the themes that I discussed earlier was around how commodity based economies such as Brazil and the Middle Eastern countries are looking to diversify into more innovative industries such as healthcare, clean technology, nanoscience, and so forth. Russia falls very much into this *State Innovator* bucket of economies and could very well be the leading player to utilize its immense resources to diversify into innovative sectors, especially life sciences.

With its vast oil resources, it has the capital needed to deploy into upgrading the country into a technology and innovation powerhouse; though, this has been somewhat muted with the recent lower oil prices and geopolitical turmoil. What Russia also has, unlike the Middle Eastern states, is a vast pool of talent, a rich history of academic excellence, and a strong university base that can be leveraged to achieve these goals.

However, Russia lacks some of the VITAL factors that may provide short-term challenges to its ambitions. One key aspect missing is the R&D infrastructure – the I of VITAL. Academic labs and research institutions have been neglected for so long that they often lack the basic equipment, let alone cutting-edge instrumentation. Even leading centres such as the Moscow State University, St Petersburg First Medical University, or Petrov Institute of Oncology are lagging far behind their western counterparts as well as many institutions in China, South Korea, and Brazil. A second missing aspect is a skilled talent base – the T of VITAL – especially returnees who have strong training in the US or Europe, specifically in the areas of biology and translational research. Unlike China, India, or South Korea, Russia still does not attract as many returnees back to their homeland. Finally, government policies and incentives – the L of VITAL – are just starting to focus on innovation and will need several years before they can start showing sustainable benefits.

One such example of government initiatives is Skolkovo. It is a new township about forty-five minutes from Moscow and is being built as the "Silicon Valley" of Russia. Similar to Singapore, the goal of Skolkovo is to be more of an innovation centre rather than to go down the path of several economic trading zones of Dubai.[22] It is an ambitious $4 Billion project intended to create high-tech centres for research and academia in biotech, IT, nanotechnology, space research, and telecommunications. Skolkovo has attracted several large multinationals in these industries to set up their R&D centres there with incentives such as tax breaks, smoother regulatory framework, and hassle-free immigration rules. But as is the case with many

---

[22] Evolution of Chinese bioclusters as a framework for investment policies in emerging markets. Ajay Gautam. *Nature Reviews Drug Discovery*. Volume 14, 8, January 2015. The paper analyses 8 bioclusters in China using academic and entrepreneurial intensity, and proposes investment policies for other emerging markets bioclusters such as Tel Aviv, Seoul, Bangalore, and Singapore among others.

such initiatives in the emerging markets, Skolkovo has been mired with delays, a less than coherent strategy, and politics, leading to an opportunity that held such a strong promise of an innovative ecosystem being potentially wasted. A high-risk, high-reward roulette!

## *Pharma Perestroika!*

After a lecture I gave at the Skolkovo Open University on 'Innovation and Entrepreneurship in the Emerging Markets', several students asked me why Russia has not been able to build a vibrant ecosystem, given its rich legacy and famous institutions. There are several inter-related aspects to that question; as is the case with the innovation ecosystems that build and evolve over long periods of time leveraging the inter-related VITAL elements. To explore this question fully, I will first delve a little bit more into the historical context of the Soviet Union from the pharmaceuticals industry perspective. During the Soviet era, most of the investments for cutting edge manufacturing plants and technology for pharmaceuticals were targeted in the now ex-Soviet satellites, such as Czech Republic, Slovakia, Croatia, Romania, and Poland. These territories were further south of the current Russian Federation and closer to Europe. The result was that these countries produced the bulk of pharmaceuticals for the Soviet Union, and post the Soviet split there were hardly any good assets in Russia since the north, including Moscow and St Petersburg, did not have high-quality manufacturing facilities. As of today, Russia is one of the few countries with high per capita GDP that has very low number of local pharmaceutical factories with good manufacturing practices (GMP). The quality standards and compliance of local manufacturers is perceived to be much lower than multinational brands, so much so that almost all of the top 10 pharmaceutical companies by revenues in Russia are multinationals and they hold ~90% market share by value and ~60% share by volume. Compare that to India where almost all of the top 10 are local companies with strong quality brands, or Brazil where the split is more of 50:50.

In contrast to current Russia, due to the strong investments during the Soviet era, ex-Soviet satellites went on to produce some leading pharmaceutical companies, such as Pliva (now part of Teva) in Croatia; Zentiva (now part of Sanofi) in Czech Republic, Slovakia, and Romania; and Polpharma in Poland. Even Stada, a global generics player founded in Dresden and now a major pharmaceutical player in Russia, was based in the former East Germany with significant Soviet influence. It is not to say that these companies became leading players only due to Soviet era investments, but it potentially did support the level of expertise and capabilities build-up. In comparison, leading Russian companies of today such as Pharmstandard and R-Pharma are less than two decades old and still not at the level of players such as Zentiva or Stada as global entities. Against that backdrop, Russia earlier this decade launched the ambitious Pharma 2020 plan to launch several new innovative products, strengthen funding for research institutions and start-ups, and incentivize local manufacturing of up to 80% of the drugs currently marketed in the country. This has prompted many multinationals to either build their own local manufacturing plants or to acquire existing facilities and upgrade them to meet the Pharma 2020 guidelines.

This market landscape should not imply that there are no strong local companies. One such example is Biocad, a leading biosimilars company in Russia with aspirations to expand into other emerging markets. Biosimilars are the equivalent of generics for biological drugs, which are based on proteins within our body and are complex to manufacture. Very few companies globally have the expertise, capabilities, and capital to launch these medicines. Since these capabilities still reside mostly in the US or Western European countries, and to an extent in select emerging markets such as South Korea, China, India, and Singapore, it is even more impressive that Biocad has been able to achieve this in Russia. An interesting aspect of my first visit to Biocad was that their office was right next to a complex with military tanks! And that's the fascinating part of Russian science and technology: this close link between the military and science, something that you also see in Israel where, coincidentally, roughly 20% of the Jewish population comprises immigrants from Russia. Most of the Russian doctors have military ranks, and the most prestigious medical schools are linked to the military, as are some key research institutions in the field of virology and infectious disease which are historical areas of strength from the Soviet era. However, while Israel has been able to leverage this interconnection between military, technology, and healthcare, specifically in the area of medical devices and digital health, Russia has lagged behind on the innovation curve.

## What's Next for Russia?

I am most intrigued by Russia of all the emerging markets. A country with such a rich history in science and mathematics, storied universities, and vast talent pool should be at the forefront of biomedical innovation. Combine that with the capital resources, efforts such as the sovereign fund Rosnano and the government-backed Russian Venture Company to fund start-ups, and Russia has most of the VITAL ingredients. But as is the case with many opportunities in Russia, this is being frittered away as well. The academic centres and universities have been neglected for far too long and there is barely much of an R&D infrastructure. Key talent often leaves Russia for more conducive environments in the US and Europe. And regional politics often plays a far more important role in distribution of funds rather than scientific or strategic merit. Nevertheless, the political will to transition towards an innovation driven economy is strong and Russia holds immense potential to be a *Future Innovator* in biomedical sciences *if* the government creates a conducive environment and implements the right investment policies.

A picture of the old city of Jerusalem.
The old city is divided into four quarters –
Jewish, Muslim (Arab), Armenian, and Christian.

# Old City, New Ventures

As you fly into Ben Gurion international airport in Tel Aviv, it's hard to miss the vast barren desert upon which this modern, high-tech country was built over the last 60 years. And as soon as you hop off the plane into the airport, you realize why they have been so successful in building an innovative country in the middle of chaos. Immigration officials greet you at the airport with some of the most modern technologies and systems used anywhere in the world. All the immigration records are digitized and upon arrival you can avail of special services that allow you to clear all border security within minutes. Given the travel restrictions between Israel and many Middle Eastern countries, the authorities even have option of not stamping the passport and giving an electronic entry/exit document to travellers. The airport can get busy and crowded due to the extra security checks at times, but still is a very efficient process.

Once you are in the centre of Tel Aviv, the infrastructure and the energy completely belie the fact that this is a place at the centre of the most volatile region in the world. The warmth and welcoming nature of the people, ever so eager to know about you and your country, about your business, their knowledge of the world and inter-dependent economies, their often-unsolicited advice on everything under the sun, all reveal the curiosity and eagerness of this nation to be a leading force in the world. The business *chutzpah* and why this country is a hotspot of entrepreneurism are well documented in the book *The Start-Up Nation*,[23] which I read prior to my first trip to Israel. And my experiences on the ground reinforced why this country is fittingly known as the start-up nation.

---

[23] The Start-up Nation: The Story of Israel's Economic Miracle (2009). Dan Senor and Saul Singer. The book analyses the reasons behind success of Israel's economy and the start-up culture.

Similar to India, Israel also provides a unique intersection of technology and tradition. Jerusalem is one of the most overwhelming cities I have ever visited in my life. I used to say the same whenever I visited Varanasi in India – the spiritualism of the place, the holy Ganges, the *sadhus* (priests) waking up early in the morning for their prayers, and the deep faith of people in this city can be immensely moving. But Varanasi is symbolic mostly with Hinduism. In Jersualem, as you walk through the Old City and across the various quarters in the Christian, Arab, Jewish, Coptic, and Armenian neighbourhoods, you are at the same time not just walking through the immense history and religious congregation in a small, compact place, but you are also trying to absorb the sheer weight of why this area has been in conflict over such a long period of time and why a resolution may just not be possible anytime soon. The city feels even more pious with the pristine white colour of the Jerusalem stone, which is the only building material allowed to be used in the city. You can sense the passion and the feeling of belonging of the various religious communities within the city, the harmony as well as the tension with which they have lived for so many years, and the vastness of cultural and economic disparities. The Jewish quarters are of course the most economically advanced and prosperous, while the Arab and Coptic quarters are languishing in poverty further demonstrating not just the religious but also the socio-economic divide of the city.

Tel Aviv, in contrast, has some of the finest beaches and offers a very vibrant nightlife, comparatively better than any city globally in my view. It is hard to believe that Israel of all places would have such energy, given the images people often see and hear on the news. The Rothschild Street in downtown Tel Aviv, the main hangout area full of restaurants, cafes, bars, and nightclubs, attract young crowds from 11pm until 5am. Israelis have such a passion for life: this ability to compartmentalize their day-to-day anxieties and tensions away from their deep desire to enjoy all that the world has to offer. Israelis are also some of the best travelled of all the people globally and this openness to various cultures, ideas, and experimentation reflects in their innovation culture as well.

Herzeliya is a small town on the coast about a 30-minute drive from downtown Tel Aviv. One of the richer neighbourhoods in Israel, Herzeliya is also a leading high-tech hub. Walking down the Herzliya Pituach, you can find offices of some of the leading global companies such as GE, Pfizer, and Siemens among others. This is also the address of Pontifax, one of the most successful venture funds of Israel. Eli Hurvitz, the late founder and CEO of Teva Pharmaceuticals, one of the largest pharmaceutical companies in the world, founded Pontifax in the early 2000s. After the death of Eli, Tomer Kariv and Ran Nussbaum have been managing Pontifax. Exceptionally visionary and dynamic life science investors, they have taken Pontifax to the heights that would have made Eli proud. Tomer, the quieter and more introspective of the two, is sharp, tuned in to the healthcare space, and heads up the partnership. Ran was part of an elite Israeli army unit before venturing into life sciences. Extremely sharp with a huge appetite for information, he quickly built a strong base in life sciences and an attractive portfolio of investments for Pontifax. Teaming up with them is Dr. Silvia Norman, one of the true leaders in Israeli life sciences, who brings a deep industry background and scientific expertise to the fund.

The Pontifax model is similar to the Momentum BioVentures business our team started in Houston – to invest in early stage technologies and discoveries from local universities and start-ups – with one huge difference in the PIPET model, the *Place*. Plus of course Eli, Tomer, Ran, and Silvia are a much smarter bunch than Chris, Upendra, Susan, and I! Herzeliya with its rich ecosystem and all the major components of VITAL in place is far more attractive a place for Pontifax than Houston was for starting Momentum.

So what is so unique about Israel as an innovation centre, especially in life sciences?

## Innovation, Pocket-sized

Israel is a very small country, with a population of only about 7-8 Million. That's less than the population of New York City and, as I often like to joke with my Israeli friends, smaller than neighbourhood pockets in China and India. But Israel consistently ranks among the highest in innovation globally. The country also has the highest number of NASDAQ listed companies outside of North America, and in fact there are more companies from Israel on NASDAQ than all of Europe combined. Israel has thoughtfully implemented most of the VITAL elements. One of the early government principles (L of VITAL) was its core focus on innovation as the centre of economic growth – something demonstrated by the 4.5% of GDP spend on R&D, the highest in the world. Israel also built high excellence universities (A of VITAL) with strong grants and funding. Consider this – the Weizmann Institute of Science has produced two Nobel laureates and several innovative drugs for multiple sclerosis and oncology in the last decade; the Technion Institute has three Nobel winners and several innovative drugs and devices during the same period; and there's strong research at Hebrew and

Tel Aviv Universities. There's ample venture funding (V of VITAL) available and exceptionally strong talent pool (T of VITAL) of scientists, managers, and entrepreneurs in Israel. A successful global pharmaceutical company in Teva further throws off experienced talent for fostering start-ups.

But one unique aspect of Israel, which has been missing in several other countries, is early stage funding. Many innovative ideas die out within the academic labs before they are ready for clinical trials or industry partnerships – a phenomenon characterized as the 'Valley of Death' – due to lack of funding for such ideas. Israel has created the Office of Chief Scientist (OCS) under the Ministry of Economy to fill this gap. The OCS is tasked with supporting high-tech R&D and entrepreneurship by providing funding programs at a very early stage of research, to progress such scientific breakthroughs to key milestones where it is ready to partner with industry. In most countries, including in the US and Europe, such funding is scarce. That's where OCS in Israel fits in – as an incubator engine and facilitator, they provide these grants and funds to help advance the discoveries through the 'Valley of Death' to a stage where they are commercially viable. A key success factor of OCS, pointed out to me in a meeting with the Chief Scientist Avi Hasson, was the de-politicization of the office, something quite different from countries such as India, Brazil, Russia, or China where state investment decisions are often driven by political factors. All investments of OCS are based on scientific and technical merit of projects, rather than any political considerations.

In the middle of a desert, in a hostile environment, and with no natural resources, Israel has built one of the finest innovation centres globally. The country now ranks among the top in several innovation and healthcare parameters – highest per capita medical device and biopharmaceutical patents, number of publications in high impact scientific journals, R&D spending as percentage of GDP, number of start-ups, and high ranking universities. All because the government was able to put in place the key components of the VITAL framework and foster a sustainable innovation ecosystem. Israel is very much a poster child of the *Future Innovator* life science cluster.[24]

---

[24]   A framework for biomedical innovation in emerging markets. *Nature Reviews Drug Discovery*. Volume 13, 646-647, September 2014. Ajay Gautam and Steve Yang. The paper analyses 11 emerging markets – China, South Korea, Israel, India, Brazil, Russia, Singapore, Poland, South Africa, Mexico, and Turkey – and proposes a framework for biomedical innovation across these markets using funding levels and R&D ecosystems as key parameters.

The small population also means that most innovative healthcare products have a rather limited market in Israel, which also explains why Israeli companies are often outward-looking from the very beginning, largely focused on the Western Europe and US markets and, increasingly, on high growth markets of China, Brazil, India, and Russia. The strength of basic research, clinical centres, and a progressive regulatory framework also means that many of the laboratory ideas in Israel can quickly move towards initial clinical testing to reach a 'proof-of-concept' stage in a relatively shorter period of time. Such a process can take many years in most emerging markets, sometimes over a decade. Medical devices and diagnostics is especially an area where Israeli companies have a strong track record of moving prototypes quickly through requisite clinical studies and getting them ready for further testing and launch in the EU or US.

Israeli companies are also adept at quickly capturing business opportunities globally. Consider the case of Protalix. In the *Start-up Samba* chapter earlier, I discussed the Brazil healthcare system and how Genzyme had built a strong business in the rare disease space by working closely with the government and patient groups. The key product of Genzyme in Brazil was imiglucerase (Cerezyme™), a drug used chronically for a life-threatening Gaucher's disease. Protalix, which was incidentally funded by Pontifax, had developed a plant-based local technology for manufacturing taliglucerase alfa (Elelyso™), an alternate treatment to Cerezyme™ for Gaucher's disease. This plant cell-based system provided high enough yield and was a much more economical process. When Genzyme ran into manufacturing problems at its facilities in the US due to contamination issues, governments across the globe, including Brazil, looked for an alternate supply for Cerezyme. Protalix stepped up. We at moksha8 pursued the company for a partnership for Brazil where we could market their product. Protalix, however, eventually went with Pfizer, a much bigger partner that could compete with Genzyme in the Brazil market. Incidentally, Elelyso™ is the first genetically engineered plant-cell based drug approved globally.

There was also another reason why Protalix targeted Brazil as a key market. Israel and Brazil shared some ethnic similarities as I had discussed previously. Gaucher's disease has a very high prevalence and incidence in the Jewish population, and Brazil with a significant Jewish population was a large market for Protalix's product.

## Networked Healthcare

The government and/or private insurance covers for most healthcare needs, placing Israel amongst the western nations in quality of healthcare. The entire population is covered by one of the four insurance companies: the majority is with Clalit which is a public insurance system; the second largest client base is with Macabi that offers better quality for someone who can afford more expensive insurance; and a couple more options. Most of the hospitals are equipped with the latest technologies, instrumentation, and state-of-the-art medical facilities. The cutting edge of Israel healthcare is further evident in a small aspect, something found rarely even in the US or Western European institutions – almost all of Israel's hospitals, medical institutions, and universities have free wifi. Now you may wonder how this impacts the quality of healthcare, but in the age of information technology with electronic medical records and handheld smart phones, Israel's doctors are probably one of the most technology-savvy physicians globally. They utilize new advances to connect better with patients and deliver high-quality services more efficiently.

One such example of what the healthcare system is attempting to achieve was evident to me on a visit with Clalit. Since it covers almost 60% of the population in Israel and has healthcare data for all its patients, Clalit is in an ideal position to understand various disease dynamics. In an experiment designed to understand the ethnic differences in the diabetes incidence across the Jewish, Arab, and Caucasian populations – the Arabs have twice as high an incidence – Clalit was studying the data across a patient pool to identify any biomarkers that can help explain or predict the incidence differences. Such data can then be used to predict diabetes trends across the ethnicities and help patients understand higher risk parameters to better manage their health. Israel is well positioned to be a leader in the new field of digital health, the convergence of healthcare and IT, by leveraging its strong expertise in both areas.

The intense focus on healthcare as a key sector for innovation is also something unique for Israel. Consider these statistics for a moment. Almost 50% of all researchers in Israel are in life sciences. Greater than 50% of venture financing annually goes into biotech, medical devices, diagnostics, and other healthcare companies. Roughly 25% of the funding from the OCS goes to biomedical sciences. There were a total of 970 life science companies in Israel as of 2013, and annually there are, on an average, more than a 100 start-ups in the healthcare space. Close to 60% of research publications are in the biomedical sciences or a related field. No other country, including western nations, comes even close to matching such a rich ecosystem.

I tried to understand this local dynamic, speaking at length with academics, business leaders, colleagues, and friends, and none more than my good friend David Goren. David moved to Tel Aviv from New York in mid-2000 as General Manager of Pfizer for Israel, and as one of the pharmaceutical leaders has been a true champion of Israeli innovation. There are elements of the Israeli innovation ecosystem covered in *The Start-up Nation*,[25] but I want to delve into it a bit based on my discussions and experience specifically for healthcare. Historically, a large portion of public R&D investments in Israel were diverted to the armed forces, which was understandable given the Israeli need to be self-reliant and competitive in military technology. Many of the business leaders, high-tech engineers, doctors, and politicians, among others, in Israel were trained within the elite army units. Apart from the military, the Israeli government early on identified information technology, high-tech, and healthcare sectors as key areas for innovation. It was also this inter-link between funding and military technology applications into electronics, IT, and medical devices early on that provided a longer-term playbook for success.

A second element has been the huge success of Teva Pharmaceuticals as a leading global player. Few other companies from Israel have a brand name as strong as Teva or a leadership position globally in their respective sector. This had the same impact on the Israel ecosystem as the success of Genentech had on San Francisco, or Biogen and Genzyme had on Boston area life science sectors. There was already a large confluence of scientific talent, venture funding, and strong government incentives available in Israel. Now there is also seasoned management and operators who periodically leave Teva to take advantage of the strong academic research and funding in Israel, and translate it into the clinic and new start-ups.

---

25  The Start-up Nation: The Story of Israel's Economic Miracle (2009). Dan Senor and Saul Singer. The book analyses the reasons behind success of Israel's economy and the start-up culture.

## What's Next for Israel?

There is no second-guessing as to which of the countries covered in this book is best positioned to be a life sciences innovation leader. I am hugely impressed by what Israel has achieved, by the entrepreneurial energy of its talent pool, coherent government policies to push biomedical research, and the world-leading academic institutions. And the tremendous advancement and coming together of such factors over the years has positioned Israel as a *Future Innovator* in life sciences. The only area Israel fumbles at times is probably also an area where it is the strongest: government incentives for life science innovation. The government is often criticized for not investing enough or investing through mechanisms, such as bio-incubators, which many on the ground feel do not provide optimal returns. But such initiatives, even if perceived as sub-optimal, have been strong catalysts in creating a thriving life sciences industry in Israel.

Terracotta warriors in Xi'an, China

# Great Wall – The Final Frontier

The first country I covered in this book is India, my country of origin. So it is only fitting that the last country I cover here is China, my adopted country for the last few years. Two countries, that couldn't be more different, yet with peculiar similarities. Both with ancient civilizations and history, with voracious appetite to reproduce, spawning over a billion each of their progenies. One that captured its economic opportunity with both hands, the other on the cusp of growth after trying hard to squander it. And both positioned to be world powers of the 21$^{st}$ century.

Towards the end of 2011, after Hocine and I closed on an investment from Eastgate Capital Group into Bio-nAbler, I started to explore my next destination. We thought of looking at acquiring or partnering with a China-based company so as to expand into this large market, which was starting to cool off from its heady days of mid-2000s. I had travelled to China, primarily Shanghai, several times since 2007 when, as part of moksha8, we had opened a representative office there (which we ultimately closed due to lack of compelling opportunities). I also visited Shanghai when Bio-nAbler, my company in the Middle East, partnered with a Chinese firm to market their products in the Middle East and North Africa region. These trips had given me a reasonable appreciation of the China market. In spite of that, when I finally decided to move to Shanghai to take a role with AstraZeneca, which had long been the #1 pharmaceutical company in China until the Pfizer-Wyeth merger, it filled me with both excitement and anxiety in looking forward to my next adventure.

And I was right. China was completely different from everywhere else I had lived, worked, or travelled to before. The language, cuisine, culture, business practices, and the sheer size of the country (even for an Indian) were beyond my imagination. Just to give an example of the scale of things in China; the Shanghai subway was built in less than a decade, and has 16 different lines (soon to be 20) laid over a distance of 450 kilometres (about 280 miles) and delivers over 2 billion rides per year. The New York subway is only 350 kilometres and delivers about 1.6 billion rides a year, and the London Tube covers 400 kilometres, delivering about 1.2 billion rides a year. And the ticket prices are about a third to a quarter of that in NY or London. Although, on the flip side, the experience of being a "sardine in a can" in the Shanghai subway during rush hours is altogether horrifying. The Beijing-Shanghai high-speed train covers over 3000 kilometres in about 5 hours. Contrast this with public transport in some other emerging markets: the Mumbai subway system that has been under planning for almost 10 years, Sao Paulo which barely has a subway system, or Mexico City where you are practically afraid to take the train. The vastly superior infrastructure of China is one of the key differentiating features of its growth versus other emerging economies such as India, Turkey, Brazil, Russia, Mexico, or Indonesia, none of which comes anywhere close to China's breadth and depth in terms of infrastructure and connectivity.

On the topic of public transport, a pro-tip on the taxis, again, if I may. They are among the cheapest in the world, and readily available in all cities across China. Given the efficient public transport system, the taxi fare has to be competitively priced and offers a fairly inexpensive way to commute around the cities. As is the case with many cities worldwide, certain automobile companies have built monopolies for the taxis in China – Volkswagen for Shanghai, Hyundai for Beijing, Nissan for Wuhan, and so forth (Hong Kong has mostly Toyota). The taxis are mostly new and clean. Do not, however, hire a dark or bright red/brown coloured taxi in Shanghai – anecdotally, the locals tell you that they will charge you significantly more than the actual fare! Go for the green, white, or blue ones instead. The low price and easy availability of taxis is probably another reason that the subway systems in major cities like Shanghai and Beijing close down from 11pm to 7am unlike the ones in New York, Paris, or London which are open until later or even throughout the night. The fact that the taxi companies are largely owned by the government and they want to ensure the profitability of the taxi companies is likely an additional reason.

Another fascinating example of such scale is the largest human migration that happens every year during the Chinese New Year holidays in the spring. I mentioned earlier how, in December 2008, the teeming streets of Mexico City felt empty and abandoned during the flu epidemic. The streets in Shanghai bear a similar look during the Chinese New Year period. Anywhere between an estimated 300-400 Million people move across the country, almost effortlessly, during this holiday week. Though a huge burden on the rail, air, and road transit system, it's nothing short of a miracle how the logistics are handled by the state. The only logistical human migration events that come anywhere close to this scale are the Kumbh Mela held every 12 years in India which brings together about 100 Million religious pilgrims to the holy city of Allahabad in northern India; or the Hajj pilgrimage to the holy city of Mecca every year where over 3 Million Muslims from across the globe travel to Saudi Arabia.

## You Are All Hired!

The sheer scale and speed of operations in China often comes as a complete shock and source of fascination to my western friends and even for folks from other large emerging markets. This is true for the healthcare industry as well. Let's consider, for example, the case of Wuxi AppTec, a leading contract research organization (CRO) in the pharmaceutical industry in China founded by Dr. Ge Li. Wuxi started as a modest company in early 2001 with a few employees and quickly grew to almost 6,000 employees and over a $1 Billion in valuation in roughly 10 years.[26] One anecdotal story of Wuxi stands out to explain such massive growth and success. As the costs of operation in Shanghai and the eastern seaboard of China started to increase over the past decade, Wuxi decided to move inland in order to capture the cost advantage as well as the pool of talent and government incentives. They chose an inland city of Wuhan that boasts of the largest student population in China, almost 1 Million strong. In order to quickly kick-start the Wuxi operations in Wuhan, the senior management went to Wuhan University and, as per the anecdote, gave a job offer to the entire chemistry class of roughly 650 students on day one, no exceptions! This would be impossible in any other part of the world but in China. For Wuxi it was a bold move that paid off handsomely, further positioning it as the leading CRO. Their Wuhan operations are now well established and contributing significantly to the overall growth of the company.

Let me share another case study, of Asymchem. During my very first trip to Beijing, I met with Dr. Hao Hong, the CEO of Asymchem. The company

---

[26] Biopharma CRO industry in China: Landscape and opportunities. *Drug Discovery Today*. Volume, 20, Issue 7, 794-798, July 2015. Christine Xia and Ajay Gautam. The paper analyses 66 China based CROs and their localization within the Chinese bioclusters.

has grown to be one of the largest suppliers of pharmaceutical raw materials in the world. Over a traditional Chinese dinner once, I chatted with Dr. Hong on how he built such a successful company. One of his key mantras was that Asymchem always hired fresh out-of-school graduates and trained them to become leaders. There are only a few hires from either multinational or competitor companies at senior positions in Asymchem to this day. If you were to reflect for a moment and think about the discipline and determination required over such a long period of time – Asymchem was founded in 1995 – to invest in employees at such an early stage and then grow them through the ranks as well as provide challenging career opportunities, it's absolutely breath-taking. And no wonder then that the turnover rate at Asymchem is in the low single digits! What's even more amazing is that this is in an industry where the turnover rate is usually as high as 25%, more so in China with a vibrant economy and vast opportunities for young talented professionals.

## Chinese Medicine, Traditional-style

The Chinese healthcare system is quite complex, mirroring the broader complexities and size of the country. It is a centralized system with large public hospitals, and most of the doctors are government employees. The Chinese government initiated an ambitious reform plan in 2009 to achieve universal healthcare by 2020, allocating $125 billion for the initial 3-year phase. This phase of reforms included expanded health insurance coverage, equalizing public health services for everyone, strengthening primary healthcare, and establishing an essential medicines program. More recently, additional reforms such as privatization of the hospital sector has further opened up the market for private players. Unlike most other emerging markets, there are hardly any stand-alone pharmacies in China with most prescriptions being filled at the hospital pharmacy. This makes the role of doctors and hospitals central to the healthcare system in China. In Brazil and Mexico, for example, a pharmacist will proactively suggest switching a prescription for a lower cost generics version. However, in China the hospital pharmacies respect the doctor's prescription and there is hardly any switching to generics, as well as low incidence of self-medication which is common in countries such as India. This centralized system is often cited as the primary reason for recent corruption scandals in the public healthcare sector. Since all the doctors are government employees and cannot practice outside of the public hospitals, there is inherent risk for bribes and corruption. The salaries of doctors average roughly $1500 a month, which is less than the salaries of sales reps of pharmaceutical companies. Hence the phenomenon of medical doctors taking up sales reps jobs at pharmaceutical companies in China. You will hardly ever find a medic accepting such a job in the US, UK, or Europe! The recent healthcare reforms in China also target this dynamics, with the doctors now being allowed to practice outside of government hospitals as well as the opening of private investments in the hospital sector.

The regulatory approval and pricing in China is also multi-layered and complex, with provincial bodies regulating such approvals apart from a national body. The regulatory framework also makes it hard for many companies to launch their drugs quickly in China. It can take several months to years just to get a clinical trial approval to initiate clinical studies in China, unlike for example in South Korea or Israel where such approvals are normally granted in less than a month. Although the government is now taking steps to ease the backlog of such approvals and introduce a more efficient system, these regulatory hurdles remain a significant hindrance to biomedical innovation in China.

Another challenge has been quality concerns for the drugs manufactured by local companies. Such concerns have allowed multinationals to enjoy strong revenue growth on the back of brand loyalty from patients and physicians. In spite of out-of-pocket dynamic of the Chinese healthcare market, most patients would prefer to take multinational brands, even if they are priced higher since there is little trust in locally manufactured drugs. Quality assurance remains one of the key concerns for the local pharmaceutical industry in China and the government is introducing stringent measures to improve the overall quality of local players. Many of the top pharmaceutical companies by revenues in the private sector segment are foreign multinationals. Even the local ones that rank in the top have a portfolio with a significant portion of traditional Chinese medicines (TCM).

This is yet another unique aspect of the Chinese healthcare market. It is the only emerging market where traditional medicines and herbal products have a large chunk of the overall market. China has put in policies as well as investments to nurture this segment and TCM companies are one of the fastest growing in China. In fact, the TCM market alone in China is worth an estimated $20 Billion, larger than the pharmaceutical markets of Mexico, India, and Turkey for example. Other countries with large indigenous natural herbs that should have capitalized on alternate therapies, such as India with its Homeopathic and Ayurveda medicine or Brazil with one of the most diverse flora, have largely lost the way on such 'nutraceutical' innovation.

## Copycat? No More

Understanding that innovation is key to the future of the country and its economy has been a central tenet of the Chinese government. Many of the VITAL elements are working in full force in China. No other nation from the emerging economies has devoted such focused investments and policy (L of VITAL) towards innovation as China, thereby putting in place foundations for being the *Future Innovator.*[27] In the 12th five-year plan of 2011-2015, the public spending on R&D stood at $600 Billion. Sure this is a small 1.5% percentage of the GDP but in absolute amount ranks very high globally (Israel, in contrast, ranks highest globally on a percentage basis with an R&D investment of roughly 4.5% of its GDP). Further, the nature of these investments also points to the seriousness of the Chinese government in fostering innovation. Most of the dollars are spent towards funding basic research at universities (A of VITAL), to build capabilities and attract talent (T of VITAL), to establish vibrant hi-tech clusters (I of VITAL) across China that can translate this research, and to foster start-ups and entrepreneurism.

But one area where China has adopted an innovative model is around talent – known as the '1000 Talent Program'. Every year, the Chinese government aims to identify 1000 Chinese nationals who grew up in China but then left to go to the US or Europe for higher education and work, and found success outside China. The Chinese government systemically identifies these individuals and invites them to return to China, to set up their research labs or start companies. This talent is often compensated at least on par with, and frequently much more, than their packages abroad and get seed funding as well as guaranteed annual grants for a period of time to help establish their academic labs or companies. This has been a tremendously successful program

---

[27]   A framework for biomedical innovation in emerging markets. *Nature Reviews Drug Discovery.* Volume 13, 646-647, September 2014. Ajay Gautam and Steve Yang. The paper analyses 11 emerging markets – China, South Korea, Israel, India, Brazil, Russia, Singapore, Poland, South Africa, Mexico, and Turkey – and proposes a framework for biomedical innovation across these markets using funding levels and R&D ecosystems as key parameters.

in attracting leading researchers and executives back to China to kick-start innovation. They have also been instrumental in building local expertise and enhancing capabilities quickly, which was then bolstered by the other key VITAL ingredients. I personally know some of the 1000 Talent Program returnees to China that have made a tremendous impact on the Chinese life sciences landscape. There is hardly any other emerging country that has taken such a structured approach to building talent and this has had a remarkable impact on the local ecosystem in China, leading to increased number of high-quality publications, patent filings, biotech start-ups, and clinical development of novel drugs.[28]

## Clustered Innovation

Let's review another element – the biotech clusters in China.[29] If you were to study the life science innovation landscape in India, you will see they are highly concentrated in a few cities such as Bangalore, Hyderabad, and Gurgaon. In Russia, it is around two cities – Moscow and St Petersburg – with Skolkovo representing an attempt to establish a new centre, but very close to Moscow nonetheless. In Brazil, again, it's primarily Sao Paulo and Rio de Janeiro. In South Korea, it is mostly Seoul, as it is primarily Istanbul in Turkey. In Mexico and Egypt, there is unfortunately none.

In contrast, China has multiple such clusters: the Zhangjiang Hi-tech Park in Shanghai, which is one of the largest R&D centres globally; the bioBay cluster in Suzhou that has built leading expertise in medical devices; the Shenzhen cluster, a leader in Bioinformatics. All of these clusters are situated on the eastern and southern seaboards. Then there is the Guangchang Hi-tech Park in Beijing

---

28  Therapeutic area 'heat map' for emerging markets. Ajay Gautam, Lily Li and Kumar Srinivasan. *Nature Reviews Drug Discovery*. Volume 14, 518-519, August 2015. The paper analyses strengths and weaknesses of 8 emerging markets – China, India, South Korea, Brazil, Russia, Turkey, South Africa, and Poland – within therapy areas of oncology, neuroscience, infectious disease, cardiovascular, metabolic, auto-immune, and respiratory diseases using start-up activity, clinical trials, and publications as key parameters.

29  Evolution of Chinese bioclusters as a framework for investment policies in the emerging markets. Ajay Gautam. *Nature Reviews Drug Discovery*. Volume 14, 8, January 2015. The paper analyses 8 bioclusters in China using academic and entrepreneurial intensity, and proposes investment policies for other emerging markets bioclusters such as Tel Aviv, Seoul, Bangalore, and Singapore, among others.

in the north; and the Chengdu-Chongqing-Wuhan triangle situated in inland China, to name just a few. Each of these clusters brings together industry, academia, funding, and talent to create a vibrant ecosystem for innovation. Consider Shanghai's Zhangjiang Hi-tech Park, one of the leading R&D hubs in the world with about 250,000 scientists, engineers, mathematicians, and physicists working in this park. All of the leading global R&D companies imaginable – from several of the Big Pharma to GE to Cisco to Microsoft and others across various industries – have set up their research centres in this park. Universities and institutions such as Fudan, Shanghai Institute of Materia Medica, ShanghaiTech, Jiao Tong, and Shanghai Institute of Biological Sciences are in close proximity for academia and industry to collaborate together, and for students and post-docs to do research in an industry setting.

It is in this aspect that China is taking an approach similar to Israel, which built expertise across the country – Weizmann Institute in Rehovot which is located inland; Tel Aviv University and a vibrant ecosystem in Tel Aviv and Herzeliya on the western coast; the Hebrew University in Jerusalem on the eastern border; the Technion – Israel Institute of Technology, and the hi-tech cluster in Haifa in the north of the country; and the Ben Gurion University cluster in the south. This breadth of innovation activity ensures that there is diversity of thought, resources, and expertise being utilized for full impact, as well as making sure the dollars being spent are not for purely intra-country regional politics (as has been argued by many, for example, in Skolkovo, Russia, or in Sao Paulo or Rio in Brazil).

The parallels with the Western world are also interesting. Old innovation powerhouses such as UK and Sweden (which amongst themselves had the major chunk of Nobel prizes in the first half of the 20th century) have largely one cluster of life science innovation each – the Cambridge-London area for the UK and the Karolinska University hub for Sweden. Contrast this with the US, which pretty much swept the Nobel prizes in the second half of the 20th century, which has clusters across the nation – in San Francisco, San Diego, New York, Boston, Research Triangle Park in North Carolina, the Seattle area, Texas Medical Centre in Houston, to name a few. Only Israel and China have replicated this breadth in their respective countries. Of course you can argue that both UK and Sweden are much smaller countries than US and China, but so is Israel which alone bagged six Nobel prizes in the last decade and has replicated the breadth of innovation across the country rather than concentrate it in just 1-2 regions or centres.

This approach from China and the sharp focus and investments in innovation is also one of the reasons why the country now has a leading position in the number of publications in prestigious journals, is witnessing fast growth in the number of patents, and numerous new start-ups in the life sciences area. Sure all this has not yet translated into a key, and probably most important, benchmark – discovery and development of truly novel drugs from Chinese labs and biotech companies. And there are continuing quality concerns that have not been completely rooted out of the system yet. But China has put all the elements in place to achieve this in the coming years and is well on its way to overcome this final frontier.

## What's Next for China?

The China juggernaut continues to roll, in spite of the slowing economy over the last few years. Of all the emerging markets, China has made the most significant progress with respect to creating an ecosystem that can foster life sciences innovation. Almost all of the VITAL elements are present in the case of China – ample venture funding, strong academic institutions, vast talent pool, state-of-the-art R&D infrastructure, and a structured, top-down government policy framework that places a premium on healthcare innovation. The long-term investments by the government are already bearing fruit, as evidenced by increasing start-up activity in life sciences and the large number of patents being filed by Chinese healthcare companies. An area where China is still lagging behind a South Korea or Israel, for example, is in the regulatory framework to facilitate speedier drug development. The government is implementing reforms to overcome this hurdle and the coming years should see more innovative drugs coming out of China firmly cementing its leading status as a *Future Innovator*.

Man and woman looking at house through frame.

# We have a dream!

Although people have different opinions on religion, cultures, languages, or cuisines, their aspirations are very similar – good jobs, education for their kids, a safe environment, and general well-being. And for people across the emerging markets such as Mexico, India, Brazil, Egypt, and even China and Russia, discussions without politics are akin to food without salt.

Here is a provocative hypothesis that I have built over the years of living in the emerging geographies. There is a social pact, so to speak, that starts to develop between the political establishment and the people over a period of time that attempts to balance the political instruments and people aspirations. And that's where the Chinese system seems to be winning hands down. Now I am sure there is going to be strong pushback for my thoughts, and there are good arguments that democracies are fundamentally better for long-term economic prosperity than a communist party regime. But for a low income, lower middle-class citizen, if you were to ask them to choose between the systems of the BRIC countries (Brazil, Russia, India, and China) as an example, my hypothesis is that most will choose the strong growth of China over the democratic chaos of say, an India or Brazil, or the communist and autocratic rule of Russia, neither of which has delivered on the dreams and aspirations of its citizens.

## People Aspirations

The Chinese social pact is quite simple yet powerful – the Communist Party will strive to provide strong economic growth and social well-being, safety, education, healthcare, and other basic needs in exchange for its citizens not interfering in the political structure. Contrast that with Russia, where one can't interfere with politics anyway but then one also does not enjoy prosperity remotely close to that of China. Or in Brazil, Mexico, or India where democratic means are available to people, but the deep-rooted corruption and cronyism belies any democratic rights and the slow economic progress leaves tens to hundreds of millions in deep poverty. If capitalism and democracy were the winners over the past decades and century, would the State Capitalism model of China be a good role model for future growth?

In my view, I find China to be one of the more open societies in the world, as opposed to conventionally held wisdom. Take safety for instance. Shanghai would rank as one of the safest cities globally, as opposed to Moscow, Delhi, or Sao Paulo, and you can often see women walking alone at 3am on the streets, something incomprehensible in most emerging markets' cities. Social liberties such as drinking, clubbing, and dating are vastly better than even cities such as Mumbai, Dubai, or Istanbul, let alone a Riyadh, Jakarta, or Cairo. Women in the workforce and at senior leadership positions also have a much stronger representation in China, as compared to most of the emerging markets. Social norms are also fairly liberal, at least in the major Chinese cities. Sure there are curbs on social media, political commentary, and certain aspects of information flow, but so is the case in many countries including Russia, as well as countries in the Middle East or Africa. And none of these places provide a counter-balance on the quality of life, infrastructure, healthcare, or economic prosperity like China. India, Indonesia, Mexico, and several other nations provide vibrant democracies but hardly any social liberties, infrastructure, or solid economic growth for the majority of the population. The tax burden in India, Brazil, Mexico, and other nations is as complex and onerous as in China, but where the Chinese population can enjoy good infrastructure, airports, trains, electricity, water, improved living and economic standards for the taxes paid, their counterparts in India, Brazil, Russia, Indonesia, and Mexico are still struggling with a crumbling infrastructure and lack of basic amenities in return for funding the office of the exchequer.

Often the stature of women in a society is also a strong indicator of future progress. In India, a daughter, unfortunately and heartbreakingly sadly, is still seen as a burden; someone who will have to be married off, for whom the family will have to pay a dowry. Equally unjust, in many Middle Eastern countries, women, even when clad in hijab, cannot be seen outside the house without a male family member, have to give up their citizenship if they marry a non-local man, and have hardly much participation either in education or the workforce. Contrast this with China, where couples are often as excited to have a daughter as they are with a son; not the least of the reasons being that the Chinese society requires a man to pay for the wedding and to own a house before proposing to and marrying a girl. Many major cities in China like Shanghai have a female-to-male ratio that is heavily skewed towards single women (hence these cities are a dream destination for single men!) This is not to say that women enjoy equal rights to men in China, and the overall female-male ratio is still heavily skewed in favour of men, on account of single child policy and male children being favoured as a result at least in semi- and non-urban cities of China. Still the progress is vastly better for Chinese women than their counterparts in many emerging markets.

Healthcare is another example. China's total healthcare expenditure is ~$375 Billion, as opposed to less than $100 Billion for India which has a comparable population. While healthcare has been identified as a key industry pillar by the Chinese government, in India it is still seen as a liability by the government. There are active, structured reforms underway in China's healthcare space as part of the new five-year plan as a response to the population's desire for better healthcare needs and partly, as discussed by various analysts, also driven by the recent corruption scandals in the industry. This includes better reimbursement, national insurance programs, broader coverage from private insurance, opening up of the hospital sector to private investors, building new hospitals and clinics in Tier 3 and 4 cities, and better regulatory framework. In India, on the other hand, healthcare reforms are largely absent and the government has an uncoordinated agenda for improving patient care, with free supply of generics touted as one big achievement by the previous cabinet, on the one hand, and the severe clampdown on the clinical and regulatory framework, on the other. The private sector in India has valiantly filled the gap, as outlined in the *It's In The Genes* chapter earlier, on back of high-quality doctors, nurses, and entrepreneurial ventures. The dynamic is similar for Mexico, Indonesia, Egypt, and other large emerging markets, where policy paralysis is hampering broader healthcare access and reforms. This is not to say that the Chinese healthcare system is ideal – there are still gaping inefficiencies and lack of access issues – but it still aims to provide better holistic care for patients than most other emerging markets.

Let's delve into the China and India debate a bit more. Although India has been a democracy for the past 65 years, the Congress Party has ruled the nation for 50-odd years. One could argue that it's no different from a single-party rule in the guise of democracy, which of course can be blamed on the deep-rooted caste system, regional politics, corruption, and nepotism in India. During the past few decades, where China grew its economy almost ten-fold to over $10 Trillion, India in contrast has only been able to achieve a GDP of $2 Trillion. In spite of a strong demographics advantage (with 65% of population below age 30); world-class educational institutions such as the Indian Institute of Science (IISc), the Indian Institute of Technology (IIT), All India Institute of Medical Sciences (AIIMS), and the Indian Institute of Management (IIM); proficiency in English language; and a strong entrepreneurial spirit, the country has woefully lagged behind China. Even in the years when the Congress Party had a clear majority rule as compared to the coalitions which were more of a norm over the past couple of decades, the country was mired in corruption and progressed extremely slow on infrastructure, manufacturing, education, healthcare, and several other aspects, not to speak of being pulled back due to the appeasement policies and initiatives. Would a stronger political will and a clear social pact with the society have been a better fuel for growth and prosperity?

A similar case emerges when you look at Brazil. For years, the economy was roiled by high rates of inflation and wild currency fluctuations. A country that is so rich in natural resources was unable to secure good governance and policies in place to leverage those very resources. The socialist policies of the government worked wonders during the commodity boom years, but left the country woefully inadequate during the years of downturn. The strong desire of the Brazilian governments to spread wealth even before it is created resulted in a lack of robust sustainable development in sharp contrast to China that has first created this wealth and is now putting in place reforms to distribute it more evenly. The study can continue for other countries such as Mexico, Russia, Indonesia, Turkey, Argentina, and several others, all with immense potential but missing one key ingredient – a strong, visionary government with a long-term view and a mutually healthy and respectful social pact with the population. Sure there has been a price to pay for such prosperity and China is struggling with its own challenges such as corruption, environmental pollution, water and food safety standards, but by and large it has still achieved a level of balanced growth for its citizens that is missing in several other emerging markets. A counter argument would be that the democratic models of Israel and South Korea are prime examples of countries that can achieve growth and social balance, but these are much smaller countries, comparatively both in terms of a geographical area and population. Most large, democratic emerging economies have struggled to emulate the Korean or Israeli models of growth.

## Political Education

In essence, a large part of this difference of China on the one hand, and other emerging geographies on the other, is the background of the politicians in public life. In China, almost the entire key functionaries in the government are well educated (largely engineers) from premier universities. If you were to look at the last few presidents in China, almost all of them are engineers from either one of the two universities – Tsinghua University (the MIT of China) or Peking University (its Harvard). Similarly, majority of the 7-member Politburo Standing Committee (it used be to 9-member committee until 2012) are engineering graduates. The larger 22-member Politburo is also filled with engineers, as are many of the provincial heads and city mayors.

Contrast this with India, where a majority of the politicians are uneducated and many have several criminal cases against them. Or in the case of Brazil or Mexico, where many of the political class are from trade unions and have not had much formal education or training. Several other countries such as Egypt (in post-Mubarak era), Indonesia, or the Philippines are a similar case study.

Further, by the time senior politicians in China become the President or the Premier or members of the Politburo, they already have had decades of experience in various aspects of public life – from running state companies to governing large provinces such as Shanghai, to tackling complex and volatile political situations such as in Tibet. By the time they reach the highest offices, they have proven their maturity and skills. Their engineering background further ensures that they are 'builders' in their thinking, hence the leading infrastructure and capabilities already in place, which is hard to see in most other emerging economies.

These centralized policies manifest themselves in the highly competitive arena of Olympic sports as well. If we were to look at the total tally of medals for some of the key emerging countries – India, Brazil, Mexico, Indonesia, Egypt, Argentina, or Venezuela, for example – the number of medals won is abysmally low for the population sizes of these countries compared to smaller nations such as Bulgaria, Hungary, Finland, and Denmark, for example. Sure there is the aspect of natural talent, access to facilities, incentives, diet, and a host of other elements at play. However, the only countries to achieve a high medals tally from emerging economies are China and Russia. Russia has been a powerhouse for many decades given the old Soviet legacy, so if we were to discount that, it is really only the China juggernaut that has had a phenomenal rise in a short span of time. Much of this has been made possible by structured thinking and government policies, investment in facilities and training their best athletes, and a strong desire to gain global prominence (and add to that the almost fanatical methods of coaching in China).

But a flipside of this structured and top-down environment is the number of Fortune 500 company CEOs. Here, the highest numbers are the Indian-origin CEOs, way more than the Chinese, Turkish, Russian, Brazilian, or any other nationality from the emerging markets. It is a similar case for non-Fortune 500 companies with Indian-origin CEOs at the helm. Some prominent current and past CEOs being Sundar Pichai at Google, Satya Nadella at Microsoft, Indira Nooyi at Pepsi, Ajit Jain at Berkshire Hathaway, Ajay Banga at MasterCard, Anshu Jain of Deutsche Bank, Victor Menezes at Diageo, Rajat Gupta of McKinsey, Vikram Pandit of Citigroup, among many others. In the healthcare industry, there's Rakesh Kapoor at Reckitt Benckiser, Rajiv de Silva at Endo, Rakesh Sachdeva at Sigma-Aldrich, among others. Further, in India, entrepreneurs and/or family owners run roughly two-thirds of companies with market capitalization in excess of $50 Million, a much higher percentage than Fortune 500 companies. Interestingly, there are an increasing number of Indian-origin deans of US business schools lately, more so than any other ethnicity, such as Nitin Nohria at Harvard, Sunil Kumar at Chicago, Soumitra Dutta at Cornell, Dipak Jain at INSEAD, among others.

So why is it that India produces hardly a dozen medals in the history of Olympics, same as the number of high-profile CEOs currently leading global companies or Deans of leading business schools? The *Wall Street Journal*[30] postulated it is a mix of various factors – education quality, comfort with English language, and willingness to move abroad given tough market environment and opportunities locally in India – that results in such a high number of Indian-origin CEOs. The focus on education and high-quality institutions in India such as IITs or IIMs are no longer an exclusive element for India – universities across many emerging markets are of high quality, and all cultures especially in East Asia drive their kids hard on education. The advantage of familiarity with the English language, often cited as a benefit for India's education system, is also starting to erode, with China especially catching up fast. So is it the chaotic, highly competitive, scrappy system of India the reason for producing talent that can manage complex, global

---

[30]    The Wall Street Journal (2014). Why India produces more CEOs than China?

businesses? And a lack of top-down, structured policies that can't tap into and groom sports talent in India? I reckon this plays a larger role than is credited with in various studies.

## Revolutionary Economics

Let me contrast a few other social pacts and political situations before revisiting the India environment. I experienced the Arab Spring in the Middle East up close – the uprisings from Cairo to Manama to Algiers to Amman to Damascus and Tripoli, and many more. One country after another disrupted decades' or in some cases centuries' old social pacts by overthrowing their leaders and demanding a more democratic model. In the middle of all this, there were (and still remain to date) two countries that were an oasis of calm – the Kingdom of Saudi Arabia and the United Arab Emirates (UAE). During the revolutions, most of my travel was confined to within these two countries since the others were quite volatile. I got to discuss with many friends, business partners, acquaintances (and taxi drivers!) the reasons why these countries have remained resistant to the ongoing struggles of their counterparts across the borders. It is a hugely complex question that I would not try to answer in simplistic terms but will share some of my discussions and observations on the ground that may help point to the reasons.

First, a little bit on the demographics of UAE. Dubai, the second largest Emirate after Abu Dhabi, has a local Emirati population of merely 15% with the rest being mostly expats from across the globe. Almost 60% of the Dubai population is from the Indian subcontinent alone. The expats have no right to vote, there is no equivalent of a permanent residency or green card process (it is also the case for other Gulf countries), no one who is not a natural Emirati can get a UAE passport, and you are not allowed to protest in groups. The situation in Abu Dhabi, the capital of UAE and the largest Emirate, is very similar to Dubai. This explains, partly, why there were no protests at all in either Dubai or Abu Dhabi.

However, there's also an element of government initiatives for the local as well as the expat population that ensured that the social pact remained intact. Dubai has been built on the promise of strong economic growth, moderate to liberal social values that attract such a large expat population, good educational institutions (at least in high school and undergraduate levels), and a high-quality infrastructure. In return, the ruling monarchy has a free hand with respect to all political decisions in the country. These promises, although shaken during the financial crises and other times in the country's history, were always strong to ensure the social contract remained in place.

Now, the UAE is a small, incredibly wealthy nation with a relatively small local population so an argument that I often hear is that this is not a good case study since the government can use its vast resources to "stem the unrest from the locals". I will, however, hasten to add that equally rich and small countries with large number of expats such as Qatar, Oman, Bahrain, and even to a certain extent Kuwait, faced a lot more tension and protests than the UAE so there are some inherent differences, some of which of course relate to the relative Shia and Sunni Muslim populations in the respective countries.

Here's a look at Saudi Arabia, a country much larger in population and size where there were modest protests that never reached a scale to threaten the monarchy. A reason often cited for this is the secretive, repressive security forces within the country, a theory that has some merit. But so were the security forces in Egypt controlled by Hosni Mubarak or in Syria by Assad or by Gaddafi in Libya. What Saudi Arabia had done much better than most other nations, similar to the UAE, was build a pact whereby the vast oil resources were being reinvested and distributed to meet the population's needs.

In Saudi, the healthcare costs for the locals are free, as is education, as well as good infrastructure, generous opportunities for jobs, and access to entrepreneurial capital. Actually, a mundane but fascinating statistic is that the state rewards you generously to get married. In UAE, for example, it can be as much as $250,000 (it's another point that, from anecdotal evidence, this money mostly gets spent on purchasing an expensive car!)

To further continue this line of argument, hypothetically, let us imagine how such a pact could have worked in at least some other Middle Eastern or northern African nations that faced the Arab Spring. Libya has the largest oil reserves in Africa, and the fifth largest in the world, with an estimated 76 Billion barrels of oil. Add to it the fact that oil extraction in Libya is one of the most inexpensive in the world, this being a major attraction for its oil fields. The entire population of the country is barely 6 Million, less than a mid-size city in most large countries globally. The country's GDP is roughly $65 Billion, almost entirely from oil exports, higher than that of countries like Sri Lanka, Bulgaria, and Kenya that have larger populations. There could have been tremendous investment potential for healthcare, education, infrastructure, technology, and so forth. Or at a bare minimum, Gaddafi could have distributed tens of thousands of dollars per year per citizen, similar to social programs in the Gulf. Maybe the outcome could have been very different had Gaddafi built such a social pact with the Libyans?

## Top-down or Bottoms-up

It is not to say that only rich nations with vast resources are able to facilitate such social instruments. Many rich nations, like some of the Gulf countries I mentioned above, failed in spite of having all the resources, as has to a large extent Russia. Other nations such as Venezuela, also with large resources, for a long time under Hugo Chavez did build a socialist pact that remained strong until his death. In Brazil, it has been a mix of socialist and capitalistic democratic principles. However, I would say that for the long-term, India provides a political structure and model that can deliver a sustained economic growth. Sure the current situation in India is a far cry from that, and the model in China has and will continue to work better over the next few years, maybe even another decade or two, but in the longer term it is the Indian model that has the potential and all the right ingredients to come out trumps.

If we were to look through history, most of the emerging economies have had revolutions and protests, often violent, but India is one of the rare countries where much of the political change has come through a democratic process without the need for violence or major upheaval. Whether it is the Arab Spring in the Middle East, the Cultural Revolution of China, or the Perestroika of Soviet Union, all of these have been deep and traumatic experiences for the respective countries. India, on the other hand, has not faced such a nation-wide trauma since its independence in 1947 in spite of the strains and tensions that a huge diversity like India presents to its social, economic, and political fabric. Most of the change has been through grass roots, democratic political processes with strong participation from the various pillars of democracy: the people, judiciary, media, and diverse political parties.

One such recent example has been the fight against corruption led by Anna Hazare, a Gandhian revolutionary. The fact that the Indian government was forced to accept many of the proposals of the movement, and the fight against corruption became central to all political discourse without the need for any large-scale violent protestations, is testament to the strength of the Indian system.

Similar is the case of India's method to tackle government ineptitude, rising youth unemployment, lack of infrastructure, dramatic slowing of the economy, poverty, women security and empowerment, amongst other issues. Many of these are the main cause of several revolutions across the emerging economies in the recent past, but were tackled in a very different way in India. Take the example of a new political outfit, the Aam Aadmi Party (AAP) or the party of the 'common man'. Within a year of starting the political party, Arvind Kejriwal was elected to be the Chief Minister of the key state of Delhi. This is pretty much unprecedented in any other country in the world including the West, much less in the emerging geographies. This 'start-up' entrepreneurial activity in the political landscape where a 1-year old party – not a spin-off or splinter group from an old party, but a true novice party – not only quickly builds a support base but also wins its very first election to form a government in the key state of Delhi was until now unimaginable. The experiment didn't work out as was planned, with the AAP losing the plot at the national level and being marginalized mostly to the Delhi region in India. But just the fact that such an experiment even took place and was enthusiastically embraced by the people is a testament of overall societal dynamics and entrepreneurial spirit.

There were several underlying issues at play – frustration of the people against corruption, economic malaise, lack of growth, ineptitude of mainstream political parties – providing AAP with an opening. But take a moment to think of it. These parameters were prevalent in many countries but only in India were such a peaceful and democratic experiment carried out – not in Egypt, Venezuela, Indonesia, Ukraine, Syria, or many other places that went through political and social upheaval in recent years. The only other places where this did happen, to a certain extent, was in Mexico where a 110-year old party was thrown out democratically at the turn of this decade, but by an opposition that was well-known and established as well; and also in Turkey where a splinter group from an old party gained power. It is this resilience and vibrancy of the Indian model that I believe could be a template for other countries in the longer term. Sure it will come with the pains of a chaotic democracy and will need tremendous fortitude and patience, but it also provides a model where the social pact is fluid and defined by the people rather than by the government.

This is why it is not as easy to say that the China model is the best as I provocatively suggested at the start of this chapter. It is a unique, top-down model that may find value in 'frontier' economies like Vietnam, Myanmar, and Cambodia with similar socio-politico-economic dynamics (although the recent elections in Myanmar and the transition to a democratic government reveals a progressive dynamic). The Indian model of democratic diversity, mired as it is in chaos in the short term, however, in my belief, has a much better long-term viability as well as the potential to serve as a template for many other emerging economies. Politics in India is bottom up, more so in the recent years. This diversity of ideas and an inclusiveness that allows people to decide how the future should look like provides it with that much more resilience. The social pact that is starting to emerge in India is of people dictating to the politicians that the elected are answerable to the public and that the Indian population will no longer be patient about corruption, incompetence, bad governance, or the inability of the political class to unlock the tremendous potential of the country.

# Epilogue

This book is an attempt to connect people aspirations and politics, and its impact on innovation, in emerging markets using healthcare industry as a backdrop. There are two big industries of political focus and reforms across the emerging geographies – education and healthcare – and I have attempted to discuss the healthcare and pharmaceutical industry in some detail in this book. And the emerging markets governments are heavily involved in both of these sectors which is a direct result of people's desires to lead healthy lives and give their children the best foundation for a productive life. The approach various countries are taking depends on their political climate and social pacts. If China is using a centralized, top-down system to create healthcare reforms and position the country as a *Future Innovator*, India is struggling on policy issues but the strong *Entre-prenovation* culture is filling the gap. Brazil and Russia are responding by using their vast capital resources from oil and natural gas as *State Innovators* to put in place policies that match people aspirations. Israel is building on its strengths to continue on the innovation curve as a *Future Innovator*. The Middle East is in the midst of using education – building strong academic centres and universities – as a pillar to step up healthcare innovation. And finally, Mexico is still seeking an innovation path where it can emulate the more successful emerging markets such as China or India. Both Mexico and the Middle East region, countries such as UAE, Saudi Arabia, and Egypt, still remain very much the innovation *Path Seekers*.

Where these countries go from here, and how they utilize their respective strengths, will again depend on the political environment and the social pacts. Consider India, for example. The new Modi government swept the 2014 national elections on back of a strong development agenda. The social pact finally moved to where the Indian population is demanding the government to deliver on the immense talent and potential of India, rather than just let

*Entre-prenovation* be the driving force. I am hopeful of many new initiatives and policies from the Modi government that will foster biomedical innovation in the coming years. In contrast, China is squarely focused on biomedical innovation as a key pillar for the future, and is in parallel implementing a huge healthcare reform across the country to distribute medical benefits to the population. Having achieved tremendous wealth creation and a large economic base over the past few decades, the Chinese government is focused on distributing this wealth to the broader sections of society. Russia is implementing the Pharma 2020 plan to foster biomedical innovation and broaden access to healthcare, and countries such as Mexico and Indonesia are broadening the health insurance coverage for their populations.

I will continue to study these markets with excitement over the coming years, with a hope that many of these countries achieve their innovation potential. Healthy populations, after all, are the best indicator of economic prosperity of a country, and the biomedical innovation emanating from the emerging markets can contribute significantly to the benefits of patients globally.

# Acknowledgments

There are innumerable entrepreneurs and colleagues who have inspired me over the years on this journey across the emerging markets, with their warm friendship, insights, and knowledge. They have welcomed me with open arms into their lives, families, and countries enriching my perspective along the way. My experiences are in many ways a reflection of their expertise – be it Steve Yang in China, David Goren in Israel, Ravi Kiron in the USA, Mario Grieco in Brazil, Hocine Sidi-Said and Alhadi Al-Wazir in the Middle East, or Elmira Safarova and Vitali Proutski in Russia.

My special thanks to Mohana Talapatra for pushing me along and inspiring me to write this book and editing the drafts several times over. Suma Nagaraj was kind enough to consider reviewing and tightening the script in the middle of her busy academic schedule. Aida Dizon reviewed several of the drafts providing invaluable guidance all along. Sam Gilpin and Birte Sebastian were the guinea pigs for the initial draft and helped confirm that it was at least readable. Special thanks to Simon Fong and Angie Loo with their help on the book cover design. Don and Natalie Frail were supportive right from the early days, egging me along to keep writing and sharing my experiences through this book. In many ways it was the encouragement and support from all of them that kept me going.

Finally, my gratitude to my parents and siblings who have been my pillar of strength all through my life, even at times when I may have doubted myself. I wouldn't be who I am or accomplished what I have without their love and sacrifices.

Printed in the United States
By Bookmasters